Wild Mama

Wild Mama

*One Woman's Quest to Live Her Best Life,
Escape Traditional Parenthood, and Travel the
World*

Carrie Visintainer

Thought Catalog Books
Brooklyn, NY

Thought Catalog Books

Published by Thought Catalog Books a division of The Thought & Expression Co., Williamsburg, Brooklyn. We publish fiction and non-fiction from emerging and established writers across all genres. Learn more at www.thoughtcatalog.com/about. For general information and submissions to Thought Catalog Books: manuscripts@thoughtcatalog.com.

Founded in 2010, Thought Catalog is a website and imprint dedicated to your ideas and stories.

ISBN 978-0-9964871-0-8
Printed in the United States of America
First Printing: November 2015
10 9 8 7 6 5 4 3 2 1

Art direction: Mark Kupasrimonkol
Cover design: Daniella Urdinlaiz
Cover photography: Noah Kalina

For Jake and Elise

Tell me, what is it you plan to do with

your one wild and precious life?

–Mary Oliver

If you don't break your ropes while you're alive,

do you think ghosts will do it after?

-Kabir

Contents

Author's Note

Some names have been changed in this book to protect the privacy of the individuals involved.

Foreword

A few months ago, I walked into the gym, dropped my two-year-old daughter off in the daycare, and ran into an acquaintance in the lobby. She grabbed my arm. "I love your Wild Mama column," she said. "You do so many adventurous things." She was probably referring to a piece I'd written about a solo trip to Rome, or the backpacking trip my family took into the mountains near our Colorado home.

Before I could respond, she added, "I used to do lots of fun things, but that was before I had kids." A pregnant pause followed. And then she said, "But that's okay. Being a mom is more important anyway. It's all I really need." The look in her eyes, tired and confused, was not convincing.

This conversation reflects a theme that comes up nearly every week in my social interactions. When women make the transition into motherhood, it becomes difficult to maintain one's sense of self. It's no wonder. Pregnancy and early motherhood are totally disorienting. Physical changes, raging hormones, and deep love for a helpless new life make it difficult to see clearly. It's easy to get lost in a whirlwind of diapers, spit-up, and endless decisions that all feel *urgent* and *important*. But sooner or later, when their children are toddlers or adolescents or somewhere in between, women find themselves asking a question that is critical for their well-being: "Wait, who the hell am I?" It's a moment of self-consciousness that can be downright terrifying, especially if the answer is buried so deep, it feels lost.

It's not only women who experience this; plenty of men do, too. Although I'm writing from a female perspective, I recognize and respect that the face of parenting is diverse, and my intention is to share my story in an inclusive way. The themes explored may even resonate with non-parents. The idea is about feeling whole as a human, and this transcends boundaries that might otherwise divide.

In reading parenting blogs, I haven't found many that are focused on a woman's identity. They discuss breastfeeding, potty training, discipline, the ups and downs of parenting, and the Mommy Wars. Occasionally there's a paragraph on five-minute self-care routines. It's useful information, perhaps, but child-centered. When *Outside Online* posted their top travel memoirs written by women in June 2012, one reader responded by asking, "Any (memoirs) by women who are also mothers? So, so hard to find."

Social psychologist Amy Cuddy stated in a TED talk that when a person loses her core identity, it leaves her powerless. People want to know: How can I honor my *self* after having kids? How can I tune in to my identity? What does it take to carve out time for my individual passions? They want role models, inspiration, and ways to take action. Many people agonize over the decision to have kids, because they view the leap into parenthood like standing at the end of the high dive.

They've watched their friends with babies transform into a foreign species who use words like "mastitis" and "playdate." Pull-ups no longer refer to exercise. Suddenly, "valet service" means wiping poop from a partially-potty-trained kid's butt. Standing there, toes curled around the edge of the board, fulfilled in their lives pre-kids, they don't know if they want to jump.

The intertwining ideas of femininity, motherhood, and identity comprise an age-old conversation. The book *Gift from the Sea*, first published in 1955, explores a woman's desire for inner harmony from the point of view of Anne Morrow Lindbergh, mother of five, who is on a solo beach vacation. She emphasizes that it is critical to women's overall well-being to carve out consistent alone time in their lives, to create, think, and simply be. It's not a frivolous luxury; it's a necessity.

Similarly, Clarissa Pinkola Estés' book *Women Who Run with the Wolves* examines the female psyche through stories and fables, and asserts that all women desire, deep down, to honor their authentic, or wild, self. Estés provides a call to action for women to reconnect with this essential part of their soul; to listen to what's inside of them, instead of subscribing to social norms that suggest doing so is selfish or superficial.

For some people, a flourishing individual identity might mean working full time, running a business, painting, sewing, cooking, volunteering in the community, training for a 10K run, or some combination of things. For me, it means travel, outdoor adventure, and writing. It took me many years to uncover my *wild*, but eventually I realized that my creativity sparks when I jump out of my comfort zone, change the scene, and meet new characters. The key is in figuring out what it means for you.

What's your wild? What makes you feel alive? How can you feel whole?

We each have our own set of gifts and challenges. In my travels, I've met mothers around the world who've found ways to honor their passions, despite their obstacles. They are single, married, or in relationships, and they come from diverse geographic locations, racial and ethnic groups, and life circumstances. The one thing they have in common is that they are all women who have figured out ways, big and small, to feel complete. It's easy to make excuses and accept a hopeless cycle, saying, "There is nothing I can do to change things," or, "I am so lost, I will never find my way back." But with effort and focus, it's possible. It's just that sometimes you may need a machete to clear the way.

Introduction: Culture Shock

Five Weeks Into Motherhood...

It's Monday morning and I'm navigating the parking lot of Walmart, a zombie behind the wheel. I've had eight hours of sleep in the last two nights, and zero showers, and the Walmart parking lot is a maze; rows of shoulder-to-shoulder cars punctuated by screaming children, harried moms, stray carts, hustling blue-smocked employees, and trolling mini vans. If the foothills of Northern Colorado weren't rising up in the west, greenish-brown humps against the piercing blue sky, grounding me in reality, I'd think I'd been plunged into a game of Pac Man. Although I don't frequent Walmart (or at least I didn't until a month ago), I have the overwhelming feeling that although the prices may be low, the risk of picking off a pedestrian before entering the store is high.

I'm taking my chances, because I just discovered we have zero remaining diapers. Actually, that's not true. There are a dozen vibrantly-colored cloth diapers sitting in the corner of our mudroom next to the hiking boots—fire engine red and egg yolk yellow and sage green—hues that looked so pretty on the website when I bought them. In that moment, I was high on pregnancy-induced hormones and imagining motherhood like a

Snuggle fabric softener advertisement, full of warm breezes and sunshine and teddy bears, and I thought it would be nice to cover my baby's bottom in organic fabric. I didn't know if I was having a boy or a girl, so I picked out a range of gender neutral colors, a whole rainbow (who says a girl can't wear red!), and clicked Pay Now.

Ironically, they got used once. (Cue: criticism from cloth diaper supporters.) Yes, I'm aware that the Diaper Battle is a tier in the overarching Mommy Wars: A battle in which well-intentioned people from both teams—Cloth or Disposable—argue in lengthy threads on the internet about which is best, citing their favorite statistics. Or they announce on Facebook if they, for instance, use cloth, posting a picture of their little Avery in an aqua heap of cloth, with a caption that says, "Cloth diapers rock!" And then a handful of people "Like" the status, and it's not until you read down to comment #5 that people begin to respectfully disagree. *Parents, start your engines*. The flurry begins. Both teams compete for support, similar to adding sponsor logos to a racecar, or picking players in a junior high kickball game.

I respect Mommy War topics because they're important personal choices: breastfeeding vs. bottle, pacifier vs. self-soothing, crib vs. co-sleeping. It's just that I try really hard not to get involved in the war part, although I admit it's tempting at times. I've chosen breast, pacifier, and none-of-the-above on sleeping arrangements (my baby, oddly, sleeps in a swing), but it could all change in a flash. Because really, I'm simply trying to survive here, which is apparent every time I look in the mirror and see the dark circles under my eyes, my tangled brown hair, the hormone-caused hyperpigmentation splotched on my forehead and cheeks like spilled paint, and the leaking milk making extremely un-sexy stars on my T-shirt over my nipples.

Regarding the disposable diapers that are #1 on my Walmart "We Need" list, my husband, Chris, and I guesstimate the water used to wash cloth diapers about equals the landfill situation from disposables. And as for covering our kid's butt in chemical-free material, well, my mom swathed both my sister and me in disposable diapers and we turned out mostly fine. Chris doesn't remember what his mom did, and he keeps forgetting to ask her, because he's not getting any more sleep than I am. But he's a twin, and I can't imagine his mother used cloth diapers, unless she was literally trying to drown herself in laundry. Which is possible.

So I guess we're on the fence, and maybe that's why we gave up on cloth so quickly. We'd been parents for less than a week when Chris looked at me, eyelids drooping, normally spiky blond hair flattened to his skull, as I accidentally threw the dirty diapers into the dryer instead of the washer. He said something like, "This is stupid. We don't need one more thing to do. I'm going out to buy plastic fucking diapers."

We go through a lot of diapers. For a beautiful creature weighing a dozen pounds and drinking only liquids, our son, Jake, sure creates a lot of waste. But it's more than diapers. There's been a growing list of "We Need" items posted on the fridge for several days, things I didn't anticipate in a million years we'd need, like mass quantities of burp cloths, a stockpile of pacifiers, a rope (or something) to tie the pacifier to Jake's onesie, a nursing bra (size: huge) and caffeinated coffee for Chris, who quit caffeine a year ago. And there's something scribbled on the paper that I can't exactly read. It might say "Foam," or "Some." With one hour to spare before Jake will be clamoring for my breast and then spitting up all over the floor, I'm forced into a level of efficiency that feels almost supernatural.

Except my superpowers are not winning me a Walmart parking spot. I do another lap around the first section of spaces, a loop that's a dozen rows wide, and there are truly no spots available. This is partly because not just one but two large SUV's are parked askew over the yellow lines, taking up two spaces each.

"Learn to park!" I yell at an innocent Ford Expedition. As for the crowds of people, everyone appears to be arriving, and no one is leaving, and I'm sure this is because the hapless consumers inside the store have long "We Need" lists too, and maybe they don't have a newborn at home, so they're taking their time, browsing the shelves, mesmerized by the amazing values, discovering things they didn't even know they needed. Which I would totally do if I weren't in my predicament. Pre-motherhood, I'd take my time gathering the items on my list, making a stop at the grocery store and coffee shop and department store.

But today it needs to be a one-stop-deal. At Walmart, I know I can get diapers, burp cloths, pacifiers, rope, a nursing bra, and coffee in thirty minutes or less. Oh, and cat food. In a rare moment of clarity, as I troll row #8, I realize the scribbled item on the list means cat food. It says Rome, the abbreviated name of our cat, Romeo. The poor guy. I fell in love with his frostbitten ears at the Humane Society in Minneapolis, where I was in graduate school, and although I adopted him immediately and adore him with the fervor of Juliet, he's been less of a priority since Jake was born. But at least we still feed him. (I tell him this is the tragedy part, and that hopefully it will be short-lived and not lethal.)

Scanning the parking lot and still finding nothing, my pulse races. I can feel sweat beading on my forehead, in my armpits, between my breasts, and under my knees. Pressing my back against the cloth seat of my sedan, I lift my butt up to adjust my skirt, which is bunched uncomfortably under the supersized dimples of my thighs. This slight movement makes my abdominals cramp, probably because I'm not really supposed to be driving a car yet. I think the doctor said six weeks, but hey, close enough. I look at the clock and see that I'm losing precious minutes. "Come on!" I say. Stopping in front of a handicapped space, I wonder if severe sleep deprivation qualifies me to park there. I hover, hands urging the wheel left. The car behind me lays on the horn. It startles me into a proper decision. *Nope, absolutely not.* I head to the far reaches of the lot, hoping for the best.

To be fair, Chris offered to go out on this errand—he's working from home a couple of mornings a week, a temporary situation he arranged with his nonprofit job—but I insisted on going. Admittedly, the nursing bra on the list didn't feel like a fair thing to ask from a man. He's supportive and sensitive, but he's still a guy. He'd have been happy to pick something out from Victoria's Secret—a lacy blue bustier or similar to announce "It's A Boy!" But the nature of the nursing bra, with its rote thick cotton beige fabric, elastic band, and plastic latch, the breastfeeding equivalent of a maxi pad, is disorienting even for me. I didn't want him to have to pick one out, and I didn't really want to own one.

But more deeply, I've adopted a pattern in early motherhood that's probably really unhealthy and possibly clinical, yet I can't seem to shake: I feel the need to do everything myself. I let Chris help with some things, but I've turned down all other help, from my mother-in-law who lives in town, and from my own parents, who offered to come from Wisconsin. Part of me simply doesn't want anyone else in my space, because I feel easily crowded, and I haven't found a way to explain this to people without them feeling offended. And part of me doesn't know exactly what to ask people to do, because it mostly seems like I'm just standing in a big pool of chaos, responding to unexpected urgent needs as they arise. Yet I know it runs deeper. In the marrow of my bones, I am adamant about doing this motherhood thing myself because I'm trying to prove I'm competent, a good mom, one of those women who can do it all. American culture loves women who do it all. They get featured in magazine articles and on TV show interviews. They attempt to run for President of the United States. I don't see why I can't be one of these women. Certainly I have what it takes.

The reality is that at the very moment Chris offered to go to Walmart, I felt like the walls were closing in around me, dripping with baby blue paint that was filling my pores. I needed to get out of the house. I wanted to experience simple things: To drive a car. Stop at a stoplight. Look at other people through my windshield. I thought maybe, just maybe, I'd stop for five minutes at the open space area near my house and put my bare feet in the river and stare at some mallards and skip a few stones: my way to connect with the natural world and the very core of my being. I wanted to walk a few steps across the sand and rocks, pretending I don't have a C-section scar that's ripped open my abdominal muscles, making it difficult for me to do no-brainer things like get out of bed, or adjust my skirt while driving a car. I wanted to be me, a woman. Nothing else. Like ten months ago, before I got pregnant, when my core was strong and my thighs were toned and I was poised to climb a mountain on foot or bike the minute the opportunity presented itself. Right now I feel like everything else except me.

Everyone—friends, relatives, strangers on the street—told me I couldn't prepare myself in advance for life with a baby. "You will enter a different world," they said, staring into space. "It will be unlike anything you have ever known." I didn't believe them. As a person who likes to embrace new experiences with an open mind, I didn't prepare myself by soliciting lots of advice. Case in point: When I decided to climb the 14,259-foot Longs Peak in Colorado's Rocky Mountain National Park, I was a teenager on vacation with my family from the Midwest. The hike is sixteen miles round trip, with almost 5,000 feet of elevation gain, but I ignored those kinds of statistics as I perused the brochure, intuitively drawn to the adventure, thinking, *Well, that looks fun! You have to leave in the middle of the night in order to summit before thunderstorms threaten in the early afternoon. What a challenge!* And also, thousands of people hike Long's Peak every year, probably even yahoos who've never set foot on a trail in their lives. How hard could it be? A few hours later, my sister and I made the trek, hopping out of our parents' minivan in the parking lot at 2 a.m. with daypacks full of peanut butter and jelly sandwiches, granola bars, and rain gear. We were both in good shape from running on our high school track team, and we'd done a lot of hiking and camping with our family, but *this* baby took us more than twelve hours, and we ran out of water halfway through, and it wasn't really that fun. We were those yahoos.

Same thing with motherhood. I chose to be "green," a little naïvely. Although I only envisioned motherhood like a Snuggle fabric softener ad a few times, and I blame hormones for that completely, my other visions were complicated. My own mother seemed happy enough as a stay-at-home mom when my sister and I were little, but I also remember her seeming overjoyed when she finally went back to college to get her teaching degree when we were adolescents. And then, I'd studied genetic counseling in graduate school, which taught me everything that could go wrong with human chromosomes and completely freaked me out about having children of my own. But I tried to stuff my reservations away into the roughly 90% of the brain matter that scientists say we don't use.

I tried to focus on what I wanted. What I thought I wanted was to simply add a child to my current life. I wanted to work, be a great mom, exercise, volunteer in the community, read books, go to movies, travel the world, hike in the woods, and hang out with my friends. When my baby was a newborn, I imagined sitting in a lawn chair in my backyard next to the fire pit, horses grazing in the field behind my house, reading a guidebook for Utah Canyon Country while my baby rolled around in a playpen. And then I imagined strapping that baby onto my back and actually hiking a canyon. Because, not wholly unlike trekking Long's Peak, lots of people do this. Millions of people take the parenthood trail. According to the 2010 census, there are 85 million mothers, and that's just in the United States.

During pregnancy, I half-heartedly read about twenty pages of the bestselling book *What to Expect When You're Expecting*, got bored with the dry, dumbed-down language and case studies, and threw it on my bookshelf next to a copy of some book about creating a birth plan, which was collecting a nice layer of dust. Deep down, I couldn't imagine that motherhood would be *that* different from my pre-baby life. I would not only do it–I would conquer.

I was terribly wrong. The last weeks have been a windstorm, and not the kind that happens outdoors when camping, which I know how to handle: secure tarp, fasten tent stakes, hide in my sleeping bag. Every day has been a foreign experience for my senses, from bright yellow poop, to silky baby skin, to spit-up on my clothes and the chair and the floor. I've endured chapped nipples from breastfeeding, kissed wiggly baby feet, learned to shower in two minutes, and gazed into the most beautiful little blue eyes on earth. If I thought I fell madly in love with Romeo in his little cage at the Humane Society, this *love* I feel for Jake runs about a trillion miles deeper. When I look at him, when I hold him, just the idea of knowing he exists, that I have a son, my very own child, evokes emotions so strong they slice through me like lightning.

Yet there are so many things I didn't expect (which are probably discussed in *What to Expect When You're Expecting*), like that Jake would cry every time I set him down. In those first days home from the hospital, I tried laying him in a bassinet, a crib, and on a play mat—every Sudden Infant Death Syndrome (SIDS)-safe surface I had in my arsenal—and then I even tried questionable surfaces like the sofa, my newly-tuned eagle eye watching to make sure he continued breathing. But without fail, within two minutes, he wasn't only breathing, he was wailing.

"What the fuck," I said to my mom friend, in a desperate phone call about how to deal with this terrifying development. What was *I* going to do if I couldn't set my baby down? In my friend's slightly maddening calm tone, she asked me three questions:

1. Was he swaddled? Sort of (it kept falling off).
2. Did I swing him? No. How could I swing him when he was lying down by his independent self?
3. Did he have a pacifier? Yes, but he kept losing it.

A few years later, just before my second child was born, I discovered the book that everyone else had gotten for their baby shower for the last several years, but I didn't know to ask for (it's another bestseller called *The Happiest Baby on the Block*) which addresses these three items, and more–a true recipe for contentment. But in my naïve state, there was no longer time for a book. Ten minutes after hanging up the phone, my friend arrived at my house with a battery-operated swing. She'd dug it out of her basement. Then she wrapped Jake in a swaddle so tight I had to reference the SIDS brochure to make sure this wasn't on the Danger list. My friend put my son, who now resembled a burrito, into the swing. She turned it on, and it swished side to side. Then, with #1 and #2 taken care of, Jake sucked on the pacifier. He sat there, eyes open. Quiet. I was shocked at how *not intuitive* that process was for me. I wouldn't have figured it out myself.

Breastfeeding was a whole different animal. My mom chose

to bottle feed (and now I see why), so she didn't have advice for me. For whatever reason, I sort of expected I'd put my baby to my breast every now and then, maybe in between yoga and typing an email. What I didn't realize is that breastfeeding would be all consuming, that it would require me to feed Jake or pump milk every few hours—a schedule that has to be maintained, without fail, in order to ensure proper milk supply and avoid engorgement, leading to possible clogged ducts or infection. And pumping milk was, hands down, the most unfeminine thing I'd ever done in my life. Nothing like smashing your nipples into suction cups, pressing the "On" button, and then listening to the mechanized hum of a machine slurping every last bit of fluid out of your mammary ducts. Breastfeeding seemed like it should be easy and natural; something women have been doing since the beginning of time. I found it difficult and confusing.

Above all, I didn't anticipate the theme of survival would be so predominant in the early days of motherhood. From the moment I walked out of the automatic sliding doors of the hospital, leaving behind the beeping machines and hovering nurses, transporting my baby to the car like a package of delicate eggs, I felt I'd been given the task of trying to keep my child alive, one hour at a time. Because along with our infant came about twenty medical brochures with a lot of bold lettering, including long lists of things to do, not to do, note, track, watch, call the doctor about, or simply ignore. There were handouts on SIDS, cradle cap, developmental stages, Shaken Baby Syndrome, feeding charts, poop logs, and newborn bathing tips. Plus, a list of support groups, in case you were feeling anything like I did: Terrified. Already overwhelmed with everything that came along with our tiny bundle of joy, I felt I also had to consider this list of "50 Ways Your Baby Might Die," and yeah, it's affected my ability to calm down.

Motherhood has been a round-the-clock job, with every emotion presenting itself in a new and super-charged state. At any given moment, I may feel overjoyed, over-tired, over-fat and over-the-top responsible, to the point that I've had nightmares that Jake is lost and tangled in the sheets of bed, and I am frantically trying to find him. These dreams are so vivid that when I snap out of them I'm literally digging around at the foot of the bed, sweating, crying, with Chris yelling my name and tugging my arm. It completely freaks Chris out, and me, and then both of us just lie there side-by-side, breathing.

At my check-ups, my midwife looks me up and down with concerned eyes. "Are you doing okay?" she's asked several times.

"Of course," I respond. *I have a healthy baby and a helpful husband and we are only a month into this gig. What right do I have to not be doing well?*

The truth is: I cry a few times a day. I obsess about everything. My brain feels fuzzy. I don't sleep when my baby sleeps. And although Chris insists on being helpful—he assists with everything from middle-of-the-night feedings to diaper changes to laundry—our interactions are often strained. Instead of making love under the sensual light of the moon, me wearing a baby blue bustier, we exchange sharp words in the dark depths of our bedroom. "It's your damn turn to feed him," one of us might snarl, or "Can't you fucking make him stop crying?" In a particularly low moment, we made a pact that we're not responsible for the words we say to each other in the middle of the night. We laughed and high fived. But deep down I wonder:

What has this baby done to us? Will I ever feel sexy again? Will we return to being a happy couple?

———————

In the Walmart parking lot, out of some stroke of divine luck, I spot an empty parking space and turn in front of a Four-Runner to nab it. Bad etiquette, I know, but I'm willing to endure a few obscene hand gestures in order to save two minutes. In fact, the woman in the Four-Runner flips me off and opens her mouth in what appears to be a long list of expletives. I wave and mouth, "Sorry," and then huddle down in my seat for a moment, hoping she'll have to park far away. Channeling James Bond, I grab a stick of gum and shove it into my mouth, chomping quickly and gazing around to see if the coast is clear. This would be an excellent time for a cigarette, I think, even though I'm a non-smoker who lights up about twice a year, and smoking while breastfeeding is definitely on the Danger list in the SIDS brochure. Despite all of this, with a quick scribble of my pen, I add Camels to the list, and I tell myself I'll store them in the glove compartment to smoke only when I'm alone and desperate, and after I quit breastfeeding, which could be tomorrow.

I take a deep breath, grab my purse, and engage the parking brake. Just as I'm about to turn off the car, my ears perk up. On the radio I hear the husky voice of Macy Gray singing one of my favorite songs from my early twenties. It catapults me back in time to the three-month period I spent living alone in Germany. I had a Macy Gray CD with me, and I listened to it over and over. She was my comfort (mostly because she spoke English) at a time when my days were uncomfortable at best.

It was my very first solo trip, but it wasn't supposed to be solo. My plan was to work in my friend's dad's office, where they needed someone to speak English. But a week before my departure, the job fell through and that was devastating because the whole trip hinged on the fact that I'd make money to cover my expenses. I pondered my options, which were few, because I'd quit my job in America and packed my suitcase. I decided to go anyway. My parents had taught me a valuable thing in life: to live within my means. I would go to Germany and figure out how to make it work.

The next six weeks were spent trying to find a room to rent and get a work permit to do *any* job. Every few days I would get up early, bike to the train station, ride the train to the *Arbeitsamt*—the employment office—wait in line, and explain my situation. The vocabulary necessary for a conversation like this is different, to say the least, than talking about the weather.

The stern woman who handled my case was clearly frustrated by the language barrier, and she often responded by repeating the same sentence, louder and louder, as if this would make me understand.

"Dieses ist die falsche form," she'd say. *"Dieses ist die falsche form!"*

Apparently I had filled out the wrong form.

My "free" time was not any easier. I remember wandering around the *Supermarkt* and staring at the boxes of soup, trying to figure out how much water to add using the metric system (1 liter = how many cups? Did I learn this in grade school?).

There was also the not-so-simple task of talking with people on the phone.

"Ah, hallo, guten tag," I'd say, into the telephone.

Silence on the other end.

"Ich bin Carrie," I'd say, introducing myself.

And then the other person would begin speaking, and I'd realize after just a few words that without non-verbal help, I was sunk. I'd slowly hang up the phone without saying, "Auf Wiedersehen."

My most embarrassing moment in Germany, which is hard to forget, happened in a pharmacy. I had to ask a male pharmacist for tampons when I didn't know the word for tampons. In this case, non-verbal communication did get me what I needed, but not without giggles from the cadre of teenagers shopping around me.

Everything I did in Germany took twice as long as it would at home, and I was ultra-focused on living frugally because the job search took longer than expected, and at the end of the day, I was exhausted from *trying* so hard.

As I listen to the final words of the Macy Gray song, I fade back into my present self, sitting in the parking lot of Walmart, and it hits me. *Oh my gosh*, I am experiencing "Germany" with Jake and Chris right now: language barriers, foreign sensory moments, a sloth-like pace every day, exhausted interactions. This is what motherhood is like for me. It's like living alone in Germany.

Although I was told that I couldn't mentally prepare for life after my baby was born, maybe that's not totally true. If someone had said to me, "Hey Carrie, remember your first month in Germany?" I would've not only remembered, but I could have tasted the soup I cooked, drawn a sketch of the woman in the employment office, and described in detail the black hair and mustache of the pharmacist who finally held up a box of tampons.

And I can recall how tired I was, how tears came at weird times, how Chris and I sometimes argued on the phone because our daily experiences were so different.

But I also remember that things eventually started clicking, and I began to gain confidence. I was granted a freelance work permit to teach English with the Berlitz Language School, and I found opportunities to truly relax—morning jogs through the park, wandering through open air markets, evenings alone on my balcony, barefoot, savoring a creamy Lindt chocolate bar—and I began to appreciate the German experience. I was really doing it. I was in Europe, living alone, making just enough money to survive. I invited Chris to join me for a couple weeks and we traveled around the country by train, checking out wonderful historic towns like Munich and Garmisch-Partenkirchen. In the end, it was the most empowering three months of my life, and it brought Chris and me closer together. When we returned to Colorado, we got engaged on one of our favorite hiking trails, in a field of wildflowers.

———

I hustle into Walmart, pondering my epiphany, and I nearly trample a two-year-old dashing toward the bubblegum machine. My highly-efficient-self has already decided how to approach my shopping list—non-food items first, finishing with coffee in the grocery section. Although even the most strategic shopping plans do not always go quickly in Walmart (the aisles are a bit like the parking lot), today goes smoothly, and before I know it I am tossing a bag of French Roast into my cart and heading toward the check-out.

On my way, I pass a display of chocolates, and I notice truffles hovering on top. They're not Lindt, but they still make me smile, back up my cart, and remember the comfortable evenings I spent in Germany eating chocolate. My shoulders soften and my face lights up. I grab a bag, tear it open, un-wrap a ball of chocolate, and place it on my tongue. I don't have time for this moment—this tiny bit of spontaneity in my fully scheduled day—but I don't care. I listen to the wrapper crinkle in my fingers as I suck on the chocolate. Warmth travels from my mouth, to my stomach, to my toes; pure, sensual joy. I stand there, tossing truffle after truffle into my mouth, oblivious to other customers, the time, my calorie intake, or whether I might get arrested by store security because I'm eating unpaid-for merchandise. I do this until there are only a few truffles left in the bag.

Finally, a tugging sensation in my breasts pulls me from my pleasant dream state—it's my signal. Must be almost time to feed Jake. I grab two more bags of truffles and toss them into my cart. They land on top of the diapers, which can't be a coincidence. "Hallo, Motherhood!" I say under my breath. As I stand in line at the check-out, I realize I've discovered, in Walmart of all places, a way to cope with this foreign new experience—not just the chocolate, but spontaneous, relaxing moments—things that make me feel like myself, which will also help me reconnect with Chris. I need to make time for them.

I'm so immersed in thinking about how this will look in my life, making mental notes in my head, that when the cashier asks me if there's anything else I need, I forget all about the cigarettes.

1

Solo on a Spare

Just Before I Got Pregnant...

As I pull into the gravel parking lot of Gold River Sales, I barely notice that the place is almost deserted. My body is moving automatically, and my mind is focused on one word: *Tire*. It's only after I have killed the engine (and my Johnny Cash CD), and I begin to roll down my window, that my surroundings slam me hard: rows of random for-sale autos, desolate highway, a billboard announcing Thermopolis, Wyoming, and a half dozen men hanging around a shabby sign that reads "Office." And now add me, a thirty-two-year-old woman wearing jeans and a white T-shirt, traveling solo on a spare tire.

My stomach tightens as I check the time: four-thirty. *Shit.* No time for nerves. There are no other options. I am nowhere near home or my destination, this is the *first day* of my road trip, I've been turned away by the only two other mechanics in town, and I'm fully aware that if Saturday is a hard day to get help, Sunday will be even worse.

The local who sent me here said, without smiling, "I guess

you can try Dave's place on the edge of town." To me it feels like this place is *falling off* the edge.

I glance up at the billboard. It shows a family frolicking in a hot spring pool. I wonder where the hot springs could be located. As far as I can tell, Thermopolis consists of scorched ridges, rock outcroppings, and sage brush.

My arrival is a distraction. The men, dressed in jeans, boots, and an array of pale work shirts, break from their slumped gathering, glance at one another, and fix their eyes on the spare tire adorning my rear passenger tire well. Nobody moves. My fingers linger on my door handle, and I catch sight of my wedding ring glimmering in the late afternoon sun. I swallow hard and tuck my hair behind my ear.

Suddenly, a skinny man in a one-piece navy blue jumpsuit appears in the doorway of the office, and he strides toward me. As he gets closer, I see that his name tag reads Dave. *Yes, Dave. Wonderful.*

But before I can speak, Dave does. "Honey, I can't help you."

I suck in my breath and stick my head out the window. "What do you mean?"

"Honey, I don't have tires that size." Dave's hair is black and slicked close to his scalp, and his skin looks like a piece of paper that has been crumpled up and then stretched taut. His eyes rove over my body. I have always wanted to be called "honey," but not like this.

"Maybe my tire can be patched," I offer, trying to sound cheerful and confident and not desperate. "I ran over something the diameter of a tent stake about thirty miles back. Will you take a look?"

Dave tries not to smile.

"The other mechanics in town turned me down."

Dave shrugs. "I'll look."

In order to dig my bum tire out of the trunk, I have to unload all of my gear for the second time today: tent, sleeping bag, food box, backpack, hiking boots, swimsuit, and towel. I try to make light conversation while everyone looks on, about my apartment in Colorado, my husband, and the hot springs that apparently exist in Thermopolis. But really I feel like I'm being forced to turn the pages of a story I don't want to tell; a story I'd like to continue. My mouth feels dry from the effort.

In the chaos, I notice that one of my backpack straps is loose (oh no, don't let my underwear fall out), and I drop my keys on the ground and run over to fasten it. Out of the corner of my eye, I see Dave pick the keys up and slip them in his shirt pocket. There is a subtle, sinister glint in his eye. My stomach tightens. Unsure what to do (what can I do?), I pretend not to notice. My story is laid out before me. I am surrounded by six strange men and a vacant lot, and it's clear that Dave has just moved his pawn and whispered, "Checkmate."

———

Ten days solo through Wyoming and Montana–that was the plan. Just me, my Subaru, and endless open road. It would be a much-needed break from my nonprofit job in a dim basement office, a chance to check out a couple of states I hadn't yet visited, and write in my journal. The mere idea of the adventure delighted my senses. A month before my departure I'd close my eyes and hear the sound of rubber skimming asphalt and the voice of Bob Dylan trembling through my speakers. I could see the sky punctuated by stars as I sat outside my tent at night sipping Fat Tire. I could taste a greasy hamburger in a diner, feel sunshine on my bare shoulders, and smell horses pawing the earth.

This trip would be all about freedom and romance and wonder. The desire for adventure had always been there, and over the years I'd found budget-friendly ways to meet the need; my time in Germany teaching English, a Spanish language immersion program in Oaxaca, Mexico, and dozens of hiking, backpacking, and canoeing trips. When I moved to Colorado after graduate school, I fell hard for the West and its symbols: evocative bluegrass music, riding horses, and irresistible cowboys like in the novel *Lonesome Dove*. I found a place to be fully alive. Colorado put me, for the first time in my life, in touch with my core; that place deep inside, where muscle meets soul, home of my most authentic self. As I stoked my core with expeditions near and far, my desire to explore and discover—to leave my comfort zone, and return—only grew stronger.

Then I got married, which was a scary step for me, considering my tendency to roam. But Chris is a man who supports, and even encourages, my independence and my adventures. From the minute we met at an outdoor concert on the University of Wisconsin-Madison terrace, where we were both undergrads, him entering the men's room, and me coming out of the women's, he embraced me.

"You're so exciting," he said, kissing me in the back booth of a bar later that night, as I told him about my plans to go rock climbing and then whitewater kayaking with the university's outdoors group.

Chris was used to women who go their own way. His mother was the only woman in his Minneapolis neighborhood who worked outside the home in the late 1970's, and she also led trips to Europe with a travel agency when he was an adolescent, leaving him and his two brothers in the care of his dad for a couple weeks at a time. This foundation in his family life made him especially open-minded, and I loved that about him. While some of my peers were in relationships with people who were possessive or protective, I was slowing falling for a guy who wasn't fazed by the idea of pioneering a one-of-a-kind partnership with me. At our wedding ceremony in the Rocky Mountains, we read vows we'd written together: "I promise to honor your dreams, because that's what makes you whole."

Really, our partnership wasn't *that* unusual. I know plenty of women who are committed to men whose lives involve danger—rock climbers, firefighters, mountaineers. Just like Chris, these women knew what they were getting in their partners, and they found them inspiring. For Chris and me, it was simply a reversal of typical cultural gender roles. I was consumed with adventure and wanderlust. He was a homebody who liked to ski and go on a camping trip every now and then. In many ways, our balance felt ideal. I'd been in relationships with artist and adventurer types and they ended badly; there was too much energy and longing, eventually exploding.

But how would this "ideal balance" play out in real life? Would Chris and I frustrate each other? Would we be content in this relationship over the long haul? I chose to focus on the possibilities. Maybe I could encourage Chris to explore even further, and he could teach me to be content close to home.

Which for him meant starting a family. He was clear about this from the start.

I'd never been gaga over babies, and then as acquaintances began having children, the reports I heard were so grim. *I don't even have time to take a shower*, they'd say. Or, *We spent $500 on a stroller*. Or, *I can't remember the last time I was alone*. I'd look at my feet during these conversations, thinking parenting sounded like the straps of a car seat—closing in around new mothers, trapping them. It seemed like adulthood contained one giant black-and-white choice: Motherhood or Adventurous Life.

Despite my reservations, I told Chris I wanted kids. All my life, I'd imagined having a baby or two, starting when I was playing house with my dolls as a child. It's just that the vision of me as a mother always loomed somewhere in the future, and I didn't necessarily consider kids a "close to home" passion. I saw them as portable and shapeable. The problem is that nothing inside me was screaming "Bring on the babies." I'd been waiting for a definitive sign.

———

In the vacant lot in Thermopolis, Dave lifts his index finger and says, "I'll be right back." He disappears toward his office, and I hope he's going to check into options for my tire. Patching, it seems, is impossible, and my tires have 16" rims, which is apparently not standard.

I want to call Chris; I need advice. But my cell phone has no service. I've been out of range most of the day, and I silently curse my phone company and their stupid promises. I didn't even want a cell phone, but Chris told me it would save my life someday.

I stand in my small sea of belongings and decide that my best strategy is to re-load. As I do this, a too-skinny man in a peach shirt with the arms cut off struts over and leans on my trunk. His shirt reads "National Cowboy Poet Gathering." He kicks at the gravel with his boots, but he doesn't speak (or lend a hand).

To cut the silence, I ask the obvious, "Are you a cowboy poet?"

He turns his head and spits. "Nope, I just went to the gathering."

"Oh." I heave my backpack into the trunk and wipe the sweat off my forehead. My packing is sloppy, and I shove things toward the back to ensure that the trunk will close. I look toward the west. The sun is hanging low in the sky, but the air doesn't feel any cooler.

The guy smiles. "Me? I'm in the movie business."

I almost laugh out loud, but then I realize he's serious, and I look away to conceal my shock. Inside I cringe. *What kind of movie business operates in Thermopolis, Wyoming?* I don't ask questions, and I hope he won't elaborate.

Just then, Dave waves at me from the office door and beckons me over. It is a welcome distraction (at this point it's all relative). I slam my trunk. The movie producer grins and rests his elbows on my car, and I can feel his eyes staring through my shirt as I walk away.

When I told people I was planning this road trip, they mostly responded with blank stares and baffled looks. Women asked things like, *Who will you talk to? Are you really going to sleep in a tent? Won't you be lonely?* Men, on the other hand, focused on the practical. *Get your oil changed. Never tell people you're alone. Keep a knife inside your tent at night.* My response was always the same: *I'll be fine. I'm good on my own.*

I spent a lot of time arranging the details of this trip. As a person who prefers spontaneity, this was not easy. But my life experience has taught me that my gender alone presents a unique vulnerability. I'd be traveling through Wyoming and Montana; "a known *man's* land," and I was not looking to get laid, or lost, so I knew a plan, even a loose one, would be better than none.

Even Chris was impressed when I sat him down to discuss my preparations.

"I'm going to drive our sedan instead of the red car," I said. "I'll be low profile, like an undercover agent."

"Good idea," he said.

"And I've got a map of my route, and lists of potential campgrounds. The oil is changed. I've got food, my cell phone, bear spray and a knife. I'll keep all my weapons in my tent at night. Oh, and I'll wear a bra."

At this, he smiled and rolled his eyes, but he seemed satisfied that I was appropriately prepared.

So I was genuinely surprised when on day one of the trip, on a two-lane highway in desolate Wyoming, I suddenly heard a clanking sound on the passenger side of my car. My first instinct was to turn up the radio and ignore it. Unfortunately, the sound didn't magically stop, so I made myself veer off onto the shoulder. The sun was hot and high, and pickup trucks were flying by like racecars. In the middle of the road, a crow was pecking at a dead rabbit.

As I stood on the passenger side of my car, listening to the air hissing out of my tire, wondering if I *really* knew how to change a flat on my own, all I could think was, "I want help, but I don't want help."

I had to make a decision. I could either try to change the tire myself and risk getting stuck halfway through, take my mountain bike off the roof rack and bike on the shoulder to the nearest town for help, or I could drive my car on the mostly flat tire and hope the next town was really close. No option was perfect. I chose to drive, and I got lucky twice: The nearest town was only a few miles away, and in that town, a nice man helped me put on the spare. Unfortunately, that may have been the end of my luck.

"Great news!" Dave is beaming. My heart leaps. Maybe he has found me a tire, and I can get on with my trip.

"There's a place in Cody that has a tire your size."

I open my mouth to say, "Wonderful!" but then my excitement fades. Cody is 80 miles away.

"You're gonna need a place to stay the next couple of nights," says Dave. "And I was thinking. Honey, why don't you stay at my place?"

I step back. "What?"

I had already accepted the fact that I wouldn't make my destination, Meeteetse, tonight but I'd certainly find a campground near Thermopolis. At this point, I was even considering the Holiday Inn.

"I've got a mansion on the river," says Dave. "It'll be just you and me, and you can set up your tent in the backyard or stay in the house. You'll be just as safe as if you were staying at your dad's place." His face wrinkles into a dirty paper bag.

My jaw drops. I am stunned that he is serious.

I know I need to remain calm. I look Dave straight in the eye.

"I doubt my dad would agree with you." I envision my father with a red face and clenched fists, standing on the lawn of my childhood home, telling me to get the hell away from these men. *Be strong*, he'd say. *And leave.* In his head, he'd strangle every last one of them with his bare hands.

Dave smirks. "Oh honey, I'm a good guy. Ask my friend here." He points to a guy about my age who looks like he wrestles bulls 24/7.

"My friend's a cop from Casper. He'll vouch for me," says Dave.

The man strides over. "Dave's okay," he says, his mouth a rope-thin line. "You'll be safe." He crosses his arms. "If you want, I can show you my badge."

I squint. "No, thanks." I can hardly believe this is happening. *Do women really fall for this stuff?* I look over at the movie producer and wonder if I've ended up on the set of some bad B-movie. But he's just standing there, leaning on my trunk, and his face is scrunched up as if he's worried.

I take another step back. The image of the dead rabbit creeps into my mind. I think about all of the bad things that could happen to me, and then I push them out of my mind, because they're too horrible. What I need to do is get out of here safely. I ponder my self-defense skills. I only know a few kicks and punches from martial arts videos and kickboxing classes. Nothing—not even a perfectly placed left hook—will protect me from this posse of men.

But I do have a voice, and an iron will. I can thank my parents for that. They gave me that gift. They taught me to speak; to stand up for myself.

I look at Dave and grab his eyes with my own. I plant my feet in the ground. "I need to head toward Cody," I state. "Can I have my keys back?"

Dave fumbles around in his pockets, as if his fingers are made of spaghetti. He chuckles like he didn't even know he had them, like he's surprised I'm asking.

"I need my keys back," I repeat.

"Oh, well, geez," Dave says. I glare at him. He gives me a disgusted look, turns away, and tosses them to me. *Asshole*, I think, but I'm nothing less than ecstatic.

As I approach my car, the movie producer waves me over. He looks me straight in the eye. "Hey, there's a campground just north of town," he says. "It's run by a very nice family. You'll be safe there."

He glances at Dave, and then back at me. Then he repeats his last sentence. "You'll be safe there."

A shiver runs down my spine, and I feel the full weight of the situation. My feet are cement, and my shoulders are lead weights. I take a deep breath.

"Thanks," I say, grasping for my door handle.

As I slide into the driver's seat, the guy walks around to my side. After locking the doors, I crack my window.

"Hey, why isn't your husband with you?" he asks.

I shrug. "Solo road trip."

He squints, as if this does not compute. "Oh."

"Well," he says. "You did good."

———

A couple of hours later, I sit at a picnic table in a campsite at the "safe campground," drinking a beer and eating a turkey sandwich. I'm still half-trembling. I leave a message for Chris that sounds fake-cheery. "I'm doing great!" I lie. "I'll see you in a week!"

I can't tell him exactly what happened until I'm home safely, because he's my *husband.* He'd probably drive all the way here just to kill and dismember Dave, and then escort me home.

Then I consider calling my parents. Somehow that need has never gone away: to dial Mom and Dad after a sticky situation and say, "I was really scared, and I'm okay."

But I don't call them, because even though I was terrified, I sense that this situation has transformed me. I feel like a bona fide grown-up. A woman. And not just any woman, but a tough, confident one.

And then something unexpected happens. As I sit on the picnic bench, chewing my food, feeling very adult, I envision myself as a mother. In my mind, I see a toddler in a green hoodie throwing rocks in a river while I recline on the shore, watching. I can't tell if it's a boy or a girl, but the scene looks happy, and I look content, and this makes me feel peaceful right this moment, sitting here in the fading light of the campground.

An image of Dave flashes through my mind, and my shoulders tense. But instead of re-living the scene in the car lot and getting angry all over again, I see that an opportunity has been presented to me. *If I have a son,* I think, *I will teach him to be better than those men. I will teach him to respect women and to be genuinely kind and caring.*

If I have a daughter, I will prepare her.

All of this feels oddly definitive, and although I wouldn't call it an epiphany, or a "beautiful vision into my future," and it is certainly not the blaring baby siren I was anticipating, it does feel like a moment of clarity. In this off-the-beaten-path kind of way, which seems to be my way, I acknowledge that yes, I do want a child. Despite everything that scares me, and all of the unknowns, I want to have the chance my parents had to raise a child, to teach him to navigate the world. I want to love my baby as much as I know my parents love me.

With that, I toss my empty beer bottle into my trunk and grab my road atlas out of my back seat. I still have a spare tire on my car, after all, and I'm going to have to alter my planned route in order to get to Cody by Monday, to pick up a new tire. I've got to re-focus. It's time to get ready for the next page of my story.

2

Under the Microscope

Halfway Through Pregnancy

I am twenty weeks pregnant, and I lie on an exam chair in a semi-dark room at the Women's Clinic, T-shirt pushed up to my bra. Sterile paper rustles under my back. For a second, the shape of my belly reminds me of an almost-full moon piercing the night, but then I remember that it is 10 o'clock in the morning, and I am simply in a windowless room with the light clicked off. Chris squeezes my hand, and I squeeze back.

"Stop worrying," he says.

"I know," I whisper, half-smiling.

He stares at the rectangular screen on the wall. "This is going to be cool."

I inhale, but my breath is not calming. The air smells like antiseptic and bleach. I think of my friends and acquaintances who have recently been pregnant. Like Chris, they've all looked forward to the twenty-week ultrasound with joyful anticipation, because it's the time when one can find out the gender, confirm the due date, and see the growing fetus. It's a phase of blissful ignorance, when the idea of parenthood is still so fresh and far away, before it all feels crushingly imminent, when one begins to ask the hard questions: Can I handle parenthood? Will I be a good mom? What if I mess up my kid for life?

But for me, things are different. There is no phase of ignorant bliss. Gender and due date seem frivolous, because of the years I spent working toward a master's degree in genetic counseling at the University of Minnesota. The memories, between the families I saw in the genetics clinic and the litany of conditions that were present in my textbooks, are still vivid. I consider the list of the fetal abnormalities the technician could detect in the next twenty minutes: congenital heart defects, spinal cord issues, cleft palate, missing fingers or toes, markers for Down Syndrome or other genetic disorders. This is just a partial list. I know there are things I've managed to forget.

In genetic terms, I'm still a relatively young woman. I haven't yet hit age thirty-five, that jagged-edged cliff the medical community labels Advanced Maternal Age, which from my experience I know isn't really a cliff at all, just a place of statistical significance. Yet it throws so many women into unnecessary states of panic. According to my genetic counseling binder, at the age of thirty-two, my chances of having a baby with Down Syndrome are 1/769, and my chances of having a baby with any chromosome abnormality are 1/323: relatively low. But the problem is I can only see the top of the fraction. No matter my age, there's always the chance of being that one. In graduate school, I only saw the *ones*. They added up to a lot of people. As much as I try to ignore it, I can't help but feel like I am under the microscope.

As a genetic counseling student, I spent much of my time looking at others under a microscope, sometimes literally. I remember one assignment in particular, in a cytogenetics lab, involving a black-and-white photo lying on my lab bench. The photo showed real chromosomes from a skin cell of a sixteen-week-old fetus extracted from the amniotic fluid of a pregnant woman. My job was to clip out the chromosomes and arrange them into numbered pairs; there are twenty-two pairs plus the X and Y chromosomes to determine the gender of the baby. The completed genetic map allowed me to search for abnormalities: an extra chromosome, a missing portion of a chromosome, a partial chromosome tacked on to another one. Sometimes the tiniest missing section of DNA, no bigger than a speck of dust on the photo, could be incompatible with life.

After a good hour, I stepped back and stared at the completed map. The chromosomes looked so beautiful, stained in dark and light bands, curved and kinked on the page. They were like ballet dancers, initiating a cascade of steps that produced every trait and every function of a living being. More than anything I wanted to know about the human created by these chromosomes. There were two X's, so this was a girl. What was her name? What did she do every day? Did she have siblings? But my job was to focus on the disorder, not the person.

After much scrutinizing, I noticed a tiny band missing on chromosome 15. According to the Internet, this was the genetic defect seen in Prader-Willi syndrome. The disorder is rare—it occurs in 1 in 12,000-15,000 births—and although the girl would have a normal life span, she'd also have mild to moderate mental retardation and feeding problems in infancy that would turn into an obsession with food as a child, and adult. She'd be at risk for morbid obesity.

Because these were real chromosomes, I knew that someone, at some point, had given the expectant parents this news; maybe a genetic counselor. I imagined a shocked look on the father's face, and tears rolling down the mother's cheeks. I considered the hopes and dreams that the parents held for this child, even at sixteen weeks gestation. I wondered if they'd continued or terminated the pregnancy. Had the fetus grown up to taste real food?

Even as a twenty-something student who was popping birth control pills every morning, the full weight of the situation settled onto my shoulders. If I were the mother, how would I cope? How would I financially support a baby with a genetic condition, which could include a long list of costs: researching and visiting different specialists around the world, medications, physical and occupational therapy, or lifelong institutionalized care? Of course, children with special needs are not one-size-fits-all. Some conditions are more serious than others, and the spectrum is long. But they all do change the game, their chromosomal alterations making up a coding system—del(5p), q27.3, CAG repeat—a language so foreign it feels like a new planet. I couldn't help pondering questions that I knew were selfish, that I couldn't bear to say out loud because I was ashamed. How does a parent remain sane in such a situation? Is there any time to be an individual? If it were me, would I even have time for an occasional bike ride? Or to write in my journal?

Years later, on a trip to Mexico, I would meet a woman named Tessa from British Columbia who had a child with Type

I diabetes. Tessa was also traveling solo, so we had dinner together, and she told me about her daughter. Either she or her partner needed to be with their daughter at all times, 24/7, because monitoring was complicated, and they had the expertise to help if something went awry. Tessa's partner supported her need for space, and they'd found a good balance. But they also needed time as a couple, maybe even more than average, because their lives were really demanding. They learned about a camp for children with diabetes. It happened the first two weeks of July each year, so they reserved this time for a vacation—just them—usually doing a home swap with people in places they wanted to visit. It was their way of reclaiming their union.

But I didn't know that in my tender early twenties. I hadn't heard of such things, mostly because I was only encountering patients in a clinical setting, in which the focus was on diagnosis and treatment. And so what happened is that my fears and questions intensified as I continued through my program, especially as I began observing and counseling patients of my own. I encountered so many unsettling disorders. One ten-year-old girl was only about as tall as a one-year-old. Her intelligence was normal, but her pixie voice and stature made her seem like a baby. Another toddler had bones so fragile he was at risk of breaking his arm if he simply tripped while playing ball. Each parent I met was focused on improving their child's quality of life, and this required complete dedication.

And then a couple of my acquaintances had babies with disorders. My neighbor gave birth to a little girl with anencephaly, a neural tube defect where the brain fails to form fully, and the skull doesn't fuse. I still remember the photo she has of her daughter: stillborn, with a sweet face, wearing a little pink cap. Another acquaintance discovered in utero that her baby had Wolf-Hirschhorn Disorder, the result of missing genetic material on chromosome 4. He died a few weeks after birth. This made the possibility of having a child with a genetic disorder seem all that much more real. If it was happening to these people, it could happen to me.

The one thing I saw in the eyes of all of these parents was love. It was a love that all-consuming. And I suspected I had the capacity to love that deeply, because of what I felt when I watched these families. My breath would stop, frozen in time, as I watched a mother touch her child's atrophied hand. Or a father and son joke about an upcoming football game, the son speaking in short, piercing bursts. Sometimes I was so moved I'd have to leave the room, where I'd go into the bathroom and stand in a stall, hands on my knees, weeping. I realized this enormous fear that was mushrooming inside of me wasn't a question about my ability to love a child with or without special needs. It wasn't even about *genetic disorders*. I was afraid of loving something that much. If I was going to be a mother, I wanted to be as good as these parents. I was terrified of the changes that come along with caring for something so deeply it can drown you.

Eventually, my studies completely overwhelmed my ability to see clearly. Although I put on a professional smile each morning when I entered the medical center, the day-to-day immersion in the world of genetic disorders became a burden for me, following me home at night and into my dreams, settling into my bones and my blood, making me question ever having children of my own. Unable to find separation between my school and private lives, I'd lie in bed at night, cuddling Romeo, wishing the sun wouldn't come up so I wouldn't have to face another day. Chris and I were still early in our relationship, and my deteriorating state of well-being threatened to cut things off before they had a chance to flourish. "I don't know what's going on with you," Chris said many times. "I don't know what to do." I didn't either. We began to see each other less and less.

One of my professors noticed this change in me and invited me into her office one day. We'd just finished a project in her cytogenetics lab, and I was rushing down the hall, hoping to fit in a run before my afternoon classes, exercise being the only thing that was keeping me somewhat sane. But my professor looked serious, and I stopped in my tracks. She opened her door, ushered me in, and told me to sit down. The chair was cool under my skirt, and her desk was cluttered with piles of papers, scientific journals, textbooks, and a photo of her two beautiful children. The minutes ticked loudly on the clock on her wall, and the fluorescent lamp felt like a spotlight. I was afraid for her to open her mouth. Had I failed a test? Done something wrong? Or maybe I'd won an award!

Running her fingers through her curly, shoulder-length hair, she looked at me for a long time. Then she said, "Carrie, I'm not seeing your best work here. And I think it's because you don't love it."

My jaw dropped and I felt my face redden. *Had she just said that?* I squirmed in my chair like a handcuffed criminal as she went on to explain the things she'd been noticing, like I appeared so pained and exhausted and seemed deflated at the end of each day. That I appeared to be simply going through the motions.

I had to admit she was right. I'd been faking it. And instead of feeling offended or like a failure, I was thrilled that someone had noticed. This woman, a brilliant scientist lauded for her research on chromosomes and aging, one of the toughest teachers in my whole program, the person everyone feared, had just announced a major new discovery: She'd seen the real me. She'd looked beyond what I was on paper—good grades and high test scores and astute lab observations—not unlike a genetic map of a person, and had seen what was going on in my heart.

When my professor saw my reaction was relief, our conversation lightened. My shoulders relaxed. Her face softened. We both took off our masks. At one point, she put her hand on top of mine. We were just two people talking. I told her what I was experiencing, and she told me what she saw when she looked at me: a lighthearted woman with a good brain and a promising future. She said she envisioned me studying literature and reading poetry barefoot on the weekends, and I laughed, because that resonated. She had articulated what I'd been feeling for years. Although I respected and admired the field of genetics, I didn't want to dedicate my life to it.

I hadn't chosen to pursue science because I was passionate about it. It was simply something I was good at in high school, and I'd heard career opportunities for women in science were exploding, and I liked the idea of busting through gender barriers. But what I really loved was English and writing, and I also got good grades in those classes, but when I mentioned I might want to pursue a creative writing degree, people said things like, "How are you going to make a living?" I didn't know the answer to that, and at the age of seventeen I wasn't self-assured enough to trust or follow my intuition, so I just shut up. I stuffed away my love for literature and followed a field of study that made good logical sense. On paper, scientific data looked much more financially promising than prose.

But the conversation with my professor, for the first time in my life, gave me permission to consider other possibilities for myself and encouraged me to explore my internal landscape. Not that it was easy, because I'd dedicated a lot of time and money (my parents' and my own) to my science education over five years, and I had no desire to throw that away. When I called my parents to tell them I was reconsidering my educational path, they were nervous. The other students in my genetic counseling program were surprised to hear me waver. Not all of my professors were supportive.

When I invited Chris to dinner and told him what had happened, he seemed just as relieved as I did. He'd been beating himself up, stumped about how to fix what was happening with me. But now we both saw that he wasn't the one who could fix it. I needed to do that. We connected deeply that evening, as I thanked him for hanging with me through this tumultuous time, and he told me how my bravery inspired him. It was a turning point in our relationship.

I took matters into my own hands. I used my voice to speak up, to talk with the head of my program. She was patient and understanding and we worked out a plan. I finished my coursework in genetics and presented my master's thesis, but I didn't do any more counseling in the medical center. Although this meant I wouldn't be a full-blown genetic counselor, I would still have a master's degree in genetics. Who knows how this might serve me in the future? Certainly, all was not lost. My years studying science had taught me a lot about discipline, critical thinking and human connection, important life skills.

Simultaneously, during my final semester of graduate school, I registered for a course on wilderness ethics, a little gift to myself. The class culminated in a winter camping trip in the Boundary Waters Canoe Area, a stunningly beautiful and isolated collection of lakes in Northern Minnesota. I found the entire experience fascinating and thrived in that setting, both in the classroom discussing philosophical quandaries around conservation and wilderness use, and in the field, where I was amazed when I actually survived outdoors for three days in sub-freezing temperatures, living in a snow cave, cross country skiing with a huge backpack on my back, and eating huge pots of oatmeal for breakfast. We laughed a lot on that trip. It was good medicine.

Also on the trip, I met a woman who was exploring the AmeriCorps VISTA program, a government-initiated effort that coordinated year-long service projects around the country for college graduates. It piqued my interest. Maybe this could provide a transition to a new career. As an AmeriCorps volunteer, which provided a small living stipend, I would be helping people, which I liked, and I could take a writing course and explore career options. Plus, I could move to a new place (Colorado) and I'd have to live simply, which would be a good challenge. When I walked off the campus of the university on the last day, I took one glance at the rows of brick buildings surrounded by green grass, and I never looked back. I closed the door on a career that was, for me, a tangle of ethics and emotions.

———

Except today in the Women's Clinic, I have re-opened that

door. A decade later, as the technician rubs the wand on my lubed-up belly, the door swings wide open. I thought maybe the emotions wouldn't re-surface, but instead it is painfully clear that there are just a few layers of skin, tissue, and fluid between my baby and the medical world. A big, scary world where, as I remembered, some things go right, but a lot of things go wrong. I consciously tried to avoid this by choosing a midwife for my prenatal care and declining all other prenatal screens: no maternal serum tests, early ultrasounds, or amniocentesis. I didn't pick up the brochures that listed various genetic disorders and how they're detected with the newest technology. I had dozens of statistics rolling around in my mind, but I forced myself to turn them around, just like they'd taught us in graduate school when we were meeting with patients in the prenatal clinic and giving results of their screens. *At the age of thirty-two*, I'd force myself to think, *my chances of having a child without a chromosome abnormality are 322/323.*

After much deliberation with Chris, we chose to accept the twenty-week ultrasound. He really wanted it. I wasn't sure. But as the one who wasn't pregnant and experiencing physical and hormonal changes, Chris wanted something to make it feel real. He was dying to see the fetus in my belly, the life growing inside me, to experience the early stages of fatherhood. I knew it was only fair to honor him with this. And a part of me wanted all of these things, too. I was just afraid.

As soon as I stepped into the waiting room of the Women's Clinic, my breakfast clogged in my throat. It was as if I'd walked through the glass doors and became flattened onto a microscope slide, frozen under the fluorescent lights. Everything about this reception area—the pale carpet, mirrored elevator, even the smell of coffee wafting from a nearby break room—brought me straight back to my desk in the genetics clinic. I wanted to run into the bathroom. This time, I didn't want to weep. I wanted to vomit.

Now, I grip the edge of my exam chair and watch the technician's facial expressions as she scans our fetus. She measures the circumference of the head and then makes a note in my chart. The corner of her mouth moves. Is that a slight smile? A grimace?

But I know the technician is trained to stay neutral. Her job is to check things thoroughly: the fetus's organs and limbs, the volume of amniotic fluid, oxygen flow through the umbilical cord. When she's finished, a doctor will come in to share observations. Her matter-of-fact nature only makes me more anxious. When she clicks on both ends of the femur to measure it, I almost scream, "What is the length? Is it normal?" A short femur is one marker for Down Syndrome.

Instead I croak, "Is everything looking all right?"

The technician doesn't look up from her wand. "I'm just making notes," she says. "The doctor…"

"Right."

"Do you want to know the sex?" she asks.

This lightens the mood. Chris and I look at each other and smile. "No," we say, simultaneously. We're in agreement on this one; we both want to be surprised. (Although admittedly, I'm tempted to look. I saw a few ultrasounds during my training and just might be able to see if there's a little penis.)

Chris squeezes my hand again, and I look at his face. His eyes are glued to the screen, like a child watching cartoons. He lets out a "Wow" as the fetus kicks a leg high and ends up in a pike position.

"A little yogi," he says, pointing. "Like mama."

I laugh. I want to share his joy. It's one of the many reasons I love Chris; he's so good at living in the present moment.

He is the reason I was able to take the leap into motherhood. After I returned home from my solo trip to Wyoming, we began talking seriously about having children. He lit up every time, and part of me shared his unclouded excitement. I, too, imagined how wondrous it would be to touch little fingers, sing lullabies, and hike in the woods with a toddler. To have a child made up completely of a combination of our genes. But as our conversations progressed, I found myself reluctant to stop birth control. Despite our healthy family histories, I couldn't help digging out my old genetic counseling notes and textbooks from dusty boxes in the basement, looking up statistics, staring at pictures of people with rare disorders. I worried about the age of my eggs.

Chris was able to shrug off the fears. "I think we just have to trust," he said, over and over, clearly becoming frustrated with me. And then he would remind me of the dozens of unknowns that exist in everyday life with or without kids: car accidents, plane crashes, heart attacks, aneurisms. He'd list things until I'd put my hand up to stop him. I knew he was right. But he didn't have to rub it in my face.

To procrastinate further, I'd give myself more reasons to stall. I'd obsess about timing. I'd think, *Maybe if I do one more trip I'll be ready. Maybe if we save a little more money we'll be ready. Probably I should visit Italy now, because if I don't, it will be another decade before I'm able to.* Chris wasn't willing to even entertain these conversations. He was done with my wallowing.

And then one Saturday morning I was riding horses in rural Colorado with a friend, the mother of a toddler, and I was feeling uncomfortable. My jeans kept riding up my ass and a mosquito bite on my hand was itching like crazy. As we crested a ridge, hazy peaks in the distance, my friend said, "So where are you at with baby stuff?"

I slumped.

"Do you want a baby or what?" she asked.

"Yeah. But I don't feel ready."

"Is Chris ready?"

"He's waiting for me."

"So what's your damn hold-up?"

I stated all the things she'd already heard.

We rode in silence for a while. I yanked at my jeans. Then she said, "You're so focused on giving stuff up, but what about the amazing new things you'll experience?"

Before I could respond, she said, "This is one of those times where you just might have to leap."

I pulled back on the reins and brought my horse to a dead stop. She was exactly right. I was holding myself back, afraid of jumping out of my comfort zone when I'm usually so brave. If I was going to do this, it was going to require the same type of courage it took for me to leave the field of genetics to pursue a different path, or to live alone in Germany. To walk a ledge on a mountain despite my fear of heights: the only way to the summit.

And then I realized what Chris and my friend could see: *I was my own obstacle.* I was only thinking about what might go wrong during pregnancy and motherhood, or what I might have to give up, but I was forgetting to look toward the depth that a baby, whatever baby I was given, might bring to my life. New experiences. Perspective. Opportunities for growth I didn't even know existed. In that moment, late morning on a Saturday, doing an activity that made me feel fully alive, I decided that now was the time to try to get pregnant.

When I got home, I rushed in the door, threw off my hat, and yelled for Chris. He came around the corner. "What's wrong?" he asked. "Did something happen?"

"Let's have sex," I said. "No condom."

The smile on his face told me he'd been waiting a long time for this moment, though he tried to seem concerned.

I threw my arms around his neck. "I'm ready. Let's do this."

We made it as far as the bedroom floor.

I was incredibly lucky. I got pregnant that first time. And during early pregnancy, Chris brought me back to my center when I started to worry. From the minute I peed on the stick and there were two pink lines, he helped me focus on the things that were under our control: good nutrition, rest, and relaxation. He's hiked trails with me, carrying all the heavy gear in his backpack, taking funny pictures of me with a daypack on my back and a growing belly in front. When he gives me foot massages, he promises me we're doing the right thing.

———

After the technician finishes her work, Chris and I sit in silence for a moment, waiting for the doctor to arrive. I shift on the table to face him, the paper crumpling under my hip. He's beaming.

"That was awesome," he says.

I smile.

"Can you believe that little heartbeat? Did you see the tiny nose?"

"Yeah," I say. "Amazing."

And I mean this. It *was* amazing to see the baby in my belly: five tiny fingers, wiggly feet, vertebrae stacked like blocks from bottom to skull. *Our baby.* In this moment, I notice a subtle change in my language. I've begun to think of our fetus as a baby. Technically, in medical terms, a fetus isn't a baby until birth, but after this experience, I see it differently. Already, my perspective is changing. I see the little human Chris and I have created together. I begin to feel the love I remember observing between parents and their children in the genetics clinic. I begin to feel like a mother.

Chris leans toward me. "Could you see the sex?"

I can't help but giggle. "No." (I really couldn't.)

As he rambles on, I find myself rubbing my hand over my belly, re-living the scan with him, wondering what the baby is doing right now. Maybe sucking a little thumb? Peeing? Flipping from side to side? I focus on Chris' voice, the details he describes. And I realize that no matter what happens in the next five minutes or five years, we will always have this moment where we got to see the early life of our baby.

When the doctor walks in, I swallow. Part of me wants to wave him away. I don't want his observations to muddy the moment. But before I know it we're shaking hands and making small talk, and then the doctor picks up the wand and starts a scan of his own.

Chris and I stare at the screen. The baby has hiccups now, the whole body pulsing in a quick rhythm. And then, with a quick brush of the wand, the doctor says, "Everything looks fine at this point." Immediately he begins a list of disclaimers, about how this is simply a screening tool, and how it is all a calculation of risk. He quotes the statistics I already know. The moment is extremely anti-climactic, and I guess that's a good thing. It all looked so much bigger in my brain, like a big glowing billboard with stars announcing our future.

I turn to look at Chris. He shrugs. "Amazing," he says.

I place my hands on the sides of my belly and hug our baby tight. Chris stands up, satisfied. He puts on his coat. "Cool," he says. "Want to grab lunch?"

I find that I no longer feel like vomiting. I actually feel like eating. After I pee.

The technician comes back into the room. She hands me a paper towel to clean off the gel and makes some notes in my chart. For the first time, I realize she's about the same age as I was when I was a genetic counseling student. I wonder how she feels about her job, and if she's better able than I was to handle the ups and downs and the stark realities of her daily routine.

She holds up a CD containing pictures of our baby. I smile. Chris and I grab for it at the same time. Our eyes meet and we laugh. "You can hold it," Chris says.

I shake my head. "No, you."

I pull my shirt down over my belly.

Chris takes the CD and beckons me over. He grabs for my

wrist. We walk out of the clinic, holding hands, the pictures secure in our intertwined fingers.

3

Checkmate

Day One of Motherhood

There is blood spurting out of my abdomen. I can see it in the mirrored lamp hanging over the operating table.

"Holy crap," I murmur.

Chris, who looks like a ghost in his scrubs, groans. He squeezes my hand. A team of doctors and nurses scurry around the white room, suctioning fluid, flipping switches and spewing quick phrases. In my drugged state, it all looks more like a theater production than a Cesarean birth. *Lights, camera, action.*

In the background, I listen to the CD I was allowed to bring in: John Denver, strumming his guitar, serenading the mountains. "Rocky Mountain High," I sing along, because I am just that cheesy, trying to keep this experience lighthearted, envisioning my belly as the mountain. I move my eyes to the lamp, trying to grasp the notion that the uncomfortable tugging sensation deep in my belly is directly related to the sliced-open flesh I see in the mirror.

The surgeon suggested in our pre-op meeting that I might

want to watch the birth. "You seem pretty tough," he said. "With all those trails you climb."

I smiled. Although I'd swelled up like an overstuffed backpack during pregnancy, in the final weeks my fingers and toes becoming the summer sausage I love to eat on the trail, it was true I'd stayed active: swimming, practicing yoga, hiking the foothills near our home, even taking a trip to a cabin in the woods at thirty-four weeks.

"And with your medical background, you might find the procedure interesting," he added.

I cringed, wishing he hadn't brought it up. The birth would be such an important day. We'd meet our new baby in the flesh, and of course, it was another opportunity for things to go right, or wrong. I hated that I thought that way.

After the twenty-week ultrasound, the uncertainty continued to torment me at times. But unexpectedly, I was often able to let go of fear completely, moved by the biological wonder of the various gestational stages, and I actually enjoyed so many things, especially as my belly blossomed and my baby wiggled around inside my uterus. Jake was the kind of baby who moved almost exclusively when I was still, which wasn't that often, so I'd carve out time for just him and me, when I'd sit down on the sofa with my book or my journal, and I'd talk to him and watch him kick and punch. "Hey there, little one," I'd say. "Come out and play." And he would. I watched in wonder as the flesh of my belly actually popped out in little peaks as he elbowed me. I'd push back, and then he'd do it again. It was a game we played.

And it's a game Jake and I still play five years later. We'll walk down a path holding hands, and when I squeeze, he squeezes back. It happens automatically. One of us will start it, and the other will follow. We've never talked about it or given it a name, and when I think about this tender communication I share with my first born, this non-verbal *I'm here, you're here; we're one*, which seemed to begin in utero, it pretty much blows me away.

———

When I was pregnant, Chris and I made a list. Not a list of all the stuff we needed for our baby, but of the things we would do after having a child. Admittedly, I prompted this. Chris was so dizzy with excitement, especially after the ultrasound, sharing the CD of photos with anyone who would watch, that he agreed. We called it our adventure list, and it included things like, *Backpack Southern Colorado. Visit an eco-resort. Check out Mexico.* I added *Sail* and *Italy* to the list, because they sounded exotic and were things I hadn't yet experienced.

Instead of spending our entire savings on a lavish Babymoon, the sister ritual to the honeymoon (or maybe it's more like a bachelor party), in which expectant parents take one final vacation before their baby arrives, a last hurrah, we started a travel fund. We couldn't afford to do both, and the Babymoon sounded so dismal anyway, like a funeral for our previous life, in which we'd prepare to be jailed for the next eighteen years. I refused to think in those terms. We knew our savings weren't going to go all that far, especially now that we'd also have to save for our child's future, but we didn't care about that. What we needed was a "holding place"—a place card that would provide means for our adventures *after* having a baby. The adventure list and travel fund served this role.

Every time I found myself drawn to buying a baby item in the store, I'd ask myself, "Do I really need that?" Because the truth is, the baby item industry is a billion-dollar affair, and a person can easily become caught up in the whirlwind while walking the aisles of Babies "R" Us, convinced they need four types of front carriers, a stroller that costs as much as a Mercedes, a hundred newborn onesies (a size which lasts about three days), shoes for an infant who doesn't walk, and nursery bedding you can't actually use, because it's on the SIDS Danger list.

As I'd walk through the aisles captivated by the entire farm of stuffed animals—horses and cows and yellow ducklings—which are also not very practical because of their SIDS risk, I'd realize the answer was very often "Probably not." Although this might seem small, these choices really added up.

———

But today in the hospital, I wonder if all of that planning and list making and saving was pointless, because our plans are already changing. I'm having a Cesarean section, due to Jake's breech presentation, which our midwife discovered, unexpectedly, at thirty-six weeks. Even after undergoing the intensely painful external cephalic version procedure, in which our surgeon laid me on an exam table, gave me drugs to relax my muscles and then pressed his hands deeply into the mound of my belly, urging and shoving in some way that made sense to him, feeling like a bulldozer to me, we couldn't get Jake to turn.

I tried to communicate with Jake using ESP, thinking, *Come on, buddy, turn!* And I tried some new-agey stuff too, lying on the ground, my pelvis tilted in the air on a ramp we made from blankets, and also doing somersaults at the local swimming pool.

But Jake didn't budge. Probably a purely positional issue, but I vaguely remembered reading in a textbook in graduate school that a percentage of babies present breech because of abnormalities. Although part of me was dying to find out, I chose not to re-read that section, because most of me didn't want to know.

What I do know is that I should be grateful for the technical prowess of my surgeon, and for the science that makes Cesarean births possible. And I am. But as I watch the surgeon plunge both gloved hands into the incision in my body, a wound that looks enormous and requires copious pain meds and antibiotics and allows me no opportunity to feel the sensations of labor, it feels like the first sign that Motherhood has announced, "So long, Adventurous Life."

The recovery will be longer now. My abdominal muscles are severed, and it will take months—or years?—to get my core strength back. How long before I can carry the baby on my own? Before I can leave the house, toting my newborn around town and up mountains and into canyons in the sling I'd placed on a hook by the back door? What if the answer is never?

———

The mood in the operating room shifts. Everyone stops where

they are, stage right or left, the surgeon center stage. Ready for the next Act.

"Chris, come on over!" exclaims the surgeon. He's smiling.

Chris lets go of my hand and takes a few steps forward. I stare hard at the reflection in the lamp above me. It appears that there is something emerging from my abdomen: a mound of red skin.

"Oh my God!" Chris exclaims. "Is that the butt?"

Someone grunts an affirmative.

Within moments, the whole baby is out. An infant is in the surgeon's hands in the air! He wiggles the baby's penis, smiling.

"A boy!" Chris announces.

I stare at the mirror, mesmerized by the little ball of wrinkled red flesh, legs sprung up in pike position because of his breech presentation, body covered in white mucous. His face scrunches up, and he wails.

"Oh," I say. "Wow."

"Carrie," scolds the surgeon. "Look away from the lamp. Look at your baby!"

I flick my eyes down.

And there, right in front of me, is our little boy. I shake my head, stunned. "Hi," I say. My breath comes in short bursts, like reaching a 12,000-foot summit with a big pack on my back. I can't believe this living being just came out of my belly—my nine-month resident is alive in the world. I stare at the umbilical cord, and notice how it still connects us. Part of me wants it to stay that way, because I kind of liked having a passenger. But now...

Everything happens fast. Chris glows at the honor of cutting the cord, and the nurses take our baby away to a corner of the room. I try to focus on positive things, like what it will feel like to hold him in my arms for the first time. But I can't help listening as they record his Apgar scores and his stats—height, weight, head circumference. I listen for any hint of concern. *Did the nurse pause in her response? Isn't a six-pound baby kind of small? What if his legs don't relax into a normal position?*

The surgeon is still working inside my body, fingers immersed in my flesh. He removes the placenta, which looks oddly like a cooked steak. Then he holds up something that looks like a large inflated latex glove. "Your uterus," he announces.

"What?"

"Yep." He laughs. "Not everyone gets to see their uterus."

"Oh."

"It's a good looking uterus, too."

I giggle uncomfortably as I stare at the delicate balloon-like object, the core of my femininity floating in the air outside my body. I try to imagine it housing my baby. Within several weeks postpartum, it will shrink back to the size of a fist.

Finally, the surgeon places my abdomen back together. This feels good, because even though I have a medical background, I'm still human, and although looking at my organs outside of my body is interesting, it's also sort of disconcerting. As he sews, I can't help but think of the children's nursery rhyme "Humpty Dumpty." I hope he put me back together correctly.

After what feels like hours, but is probably only ten minutes, a nurse wraps my baby in a blanket and places him on my chest. "He's beautiful," she says.

I stare into his eyes and take in his sparse dark hair and rosebud mouth.

Chris kisses me on the forehead. "Good job, Mama," he says. His eyes are watery with emotion. "You're amazing."

I smile. "You too."

He looks at our baby's face. "Doesn't he look like a Jake?"

I bite my upper lip. Somehow, he really does. I nod.

"Jake Owen," says Chris.

"Jake Owen," I repeat.

As I stroke Jake's tiny forehead with my thumb, I say, "Hi sweetheart. Hi Jake." A rush, like an avalanche, pulses through me—a feeling I've never experienced before. Is it love? Enormous responsibility? Joy laced with fear? I feel stunned by the moment, my every cell tuned in to the needs of this tiny creature. Under the weight of my new baby, his six pounds directly over my heart, I think I might lie in this position forever. This might be all the adventure I need.

4

American Dream

Seven Weeks into Motherhood

I didn't see the crevasse coming.

It's a sunny Wednesday morning, and I'm driving my sedan, shaky with exhaustion, my passenger seat overwhelmed with baggage; a diaper tote bursting with baby gear, a nine-foot-long cloth Moby Wrap, and a messenger bag spewing pens, manila folders, and business cards. Jake is asleep in the backseat. I lift a diet soda from my cup holder and take a long swig, hating the taste of chemical fake sugar, frustrated that caffeine in any form has become my addiction during this phase of survival. As I squint through the windshield, I notice the sunshine is strong and the sky is blue, a combination that practically sings a melody or strums a banjo, beckoning me into the outdoors.

But today it only reminds me that I've forgotten my sunglasses. "Damn," I say, but I don't have the energy to turn the car around. My entire body hurts. The inventory is long—my back aches and a crook in my neck sends pain all the way down to my left hip—and there's more. But instead I focus on Jake, who fell asleep in his car seat the minute I hit reverse in my driveway. Listening for any sound coming from his little bow-shaped mouth, I head toward a place that used to be comfortable: my office.

Seven weeks postpartum, I'm on my way to "having it all," returning to work at the nonprofit that's employed me since I completed my AmeriCorps service. It's a job in which I've been successful: complimented for my skill time and again, and even offered the position of executive director. But I turned down the promotion. In another decision viewed as illogical by others, I declined, citing some vague thing about not being ready, which was true. The reason I wasn't ready is I still wanted to be a writer. And I'd taken steps toward accomplishing this. Unable to stomach the expense of a formal English degree, I'd filled my free time with low cost educational resources, auditioning and getting accepted into a critique group and taking a continuing education course in creative writing. My first short story was accepted for publication. During pregnancy, I spent hours in my chair practicing my craft, and also researching the business. It turned out there was even a field of science writing, and I was working toward joining a professional association. I'd been offered my first freelance project by a local magazine. Things were looking good.

Except now nothing is looking good, because I can't see more than three feet in front of my face, my entire life socked in by fog, like a dismal version of the cloud forest Chris and I visited in Costa Rica on our honeymoon. Jake stirs in the backseat, and with a glance into the rearview window, I notice he's doing his little "Rabbit Dance"—a series of body movements that means he's fast asleep. His eyelids and lips twitch, and his arms and legs jiggle as if he's running. Chris and I joke that when he does this, maybe he's having a dream about chasing rabbits. It's adorable, something I love him to do when he's asleep in my arms in my nursing chair, so I can observe every little wrinkle of his face and fingers. But watching now in the mirror only makes my shoulders tense and my hands grip the steering wheel, which makes them shake even harder, because I know I'll have to wake him up prematurely in a few minutes when I park my car. Which means he'll cry. And won't go back to sleep.

I pass the intersection where I can either turn toward Walmart or head straight to my office, and I think of how many times Chris or I have been to that Super Center in the last couple weeks, since my first trip when I couldn't find a parking space. Despite our best efforts, the We Need list keeps outgrowing the paper, just like Jake and his onesies, and Walmart really is a good place to get everything. They even have bike tubes. Who knew?

Not that I've been riding my bike, because my entire core still feels dead, and I can't lift my right leg over the frame. But one day while Jake was napping I found a kid bike trailer for sale on Craigslist, the owner saying they'd strapped their infant's car seat inside, and in a burst of optimism, I went out to the garage to see if my bike had the right attachments.

Unfortunately, I found a flat tire. This made me sigh, and then scream, "Dammit!" The symbolism pushed me over an edge, a threshold I'd been approaching with fervor despite my best efforts to melt into motherhood, my imminent return to work fueling the fire. It threw me into a tantrum so irrational yet uncontrollable I worried that my neighbors, with whom we share a gravel driveway, might notice. But I didn't care. I sat on the cement floor of the garage in a big heap of my own flab, cursing and kicking the ground. And then I stood up and flung a wrench at the canoe, which ricocheted and clunked into the handle of the lawnmower. I pushed my bike on its side. I walked up to the wall and banged it with the outside of my fist, gaining momentum, and then punching and flailing and biting my bottom lip until I could taste blood. *What is wrong with me?* I thought. *I am a strong woman. I have a healthy baby and a helpful husband. Why is motherhood so hard?*

And then I walked out, pulled down the garage door, letting it slam shut, went into the house and wrote Bike Tube on the We Need list. I emailed the guy on Craigslist and said I wanted to buy the (fucking) bike trailer, and told him my husband would stop by on the way home from work, cash in hand. When Chris texted me and said, "Um, explain?" I texted back, "Just do it."

That night, Chris came home with the bike trailer, but he was pissed. "What is wrong with you?" he asked. "Why do we need this for a newborn?"

"Nothing is *wrong* with me. I am trying to live normally," I said.

While I strapped Jake into his car seat that evening, and then into the bike trailer, just to see the set-up, Chris ignored me. He sat in the TV room watching sports and drinking a beer. He slept on the sofa that night.

Once the house was quiet, Jake asleep for one of his two-hour increments, I did yet another thing I never anticipated I'd do in my life. I got on my computer and typed in "Postpartum Depression." My tantrum in the garage had shaken me. I've never responded to anything with that degree of rage in my entire life, even when faced with poorly-intentioned cowboys in the Middle of Nowhere, Wyoming. Instead of motherhood getting easier, I was feeling less like myself every day.

But instead of reading a medical site that listed the clinical signs and symptoms of postpartum depression, I was drawn to a news story about a woman who had drowned her baby in a bathtub, the result of mental health issues, including depression. *I've never wanted to do anything that serious*, I thought. The worst I could think of was a few times when I'd wanted to shake Jake to stop his crying. Instead I'd left the room and taken some deep breaths, and cried myself. And although I was still dreaming about losing Jake in the sheets of the bed, often waking up covered in sweat, I had no intention of hurting my baby. I shut down my computer, deciding postpartum depression wasn't me.

———

As I near my office, I remember there are no viable parking spots within a few blocks of the front door, because it's located in the heart of Fort Collins, the charming town center that's full of specialty shops and restaurants with patios, a place where people come on vacation because it keeps making "Best Places to Live" lists. There's a two-hour parking limit. Pre-pregnancy, that was never a big deal. Sometimes I'd even bike the five miles into town, or I'd choose a spot four blocks away and enjoy the few extra moments of fresh air.

Today, four blocks feels like four miles, an unsurmountable peak given my poorly packed gear and extra passenger. Hesitating to turn off the car, because I know Jake will wake up the minute the engine stops vibrating, I sit in the spot on the edge of the tree-lined street, car humming. I place my hands in my lap and drop my head to my chin. Without warning, tears come. They roll down my face and drip onto my nursing shirt, which has ruffled flaps of cloth that open easily for discreet breastfeeding, and looked gorgeous on the model online, but makes me look like a costumed whale, complete with dark splatters of spit-up that I forgot to wash out. All I want to do is go home. Or give up.

My job didn't provide paid maternity leave, so I took off as much time as Chris and I felt we could afford. Toward the middle of my pregnancy, we sat down with a handheld calculator and notebook, crunching numbers. As I wrote down our income and expenses in two separate columns, watching the expense list get unsettlingly long, I thought about how crazy it seemed to be doing this—how in America it's atypical for women to receive paid maternity leave, and if they do, it's rarely more than a few weeks. In doing further research, I read that the United States is one of only four countries in the world that doesn't have a national law mandating paid time off for new parents. (The others are Lesotho, Papua New Guinea, and Swaziland.)

Why is it that virtually every other country in the world respects the huge change that parenthood brings, offering mothers (and sometimes fathers) many weeks or months of paid time off, but in America it's expected that new parents either save money in order to take up to the three months of unpaid leave required by the Family Medical Leave Act, or keep working like nothing's happened? I, as well as everyone I knew, made extensive plans for my maternity leave in advance, feeling guilty, as if I was abandoning the most important tasks in the world, divvying out my workload and agreeing to still be in contact by email, and feeling the need to promise that not only would I be back after my baby was born, I'd be back with renewed focus, ready to work harder than ever to make up for lost time.

One woman I know, Meredith, did it differently. She took full advantage of her maternity leave by booking a trip to Spain. She figured, Why not? When else am I going to take three months off of work? Her husband's law firm was not supportive of the decision to take that long of a leave, but they tolerated it. So Meredith and her husband saved money and skipped the Babymoon, and a few weeks after their infant was born, they flew to Europe, holed up in a town with cobblestone streets, and let adoring local women admire their family and hold their baby every day. They had the foresight to make plans to visit a new place—one that's known for especially treasuring children—and by doing so had a true immersion experience, much more than a vacation, the kind of scenario most of us crave.

Although I think it's a fabulous idea now, I didn't think of it at that time. I was too focused on planning, caught up inside my own box. For my maternity leave, I used up all of the vacation time I'd accrued at my job and was able to tack on a few more unpaid weeks, creating a whopping seven-week *siesta* for me and my newborn. Chris would take off two weeks from his nonprofit job and then go back full time. Out of some combination of hope and desperation, I crossed my fingers that new motherhood would truly be more like a fabric softener ad, and less like the way other women described it. Every time I did this, I felt a pit grow in my stomach, burgeoning alongside the growing baby in my uterus, clear foreshadowing.

In theory, I was fortunate. My boss, a father of several grown children, presented me with an ideal situation for returning to work: I could bring my baby with me. When I was in my third trimester of pregnancy, we sat on the brick patio outside of our office and discussed exactly what this would look like. The conversation felt about as foreign as showing pictures of a trip to Antarctica *before the trip actually happened*. Nonetheless, as the leader of the organization, I understood his need to plan, and I felt lucky that he was enthusiastic about my return, and was offering me an arrangement that felt progressive, at least in America.

He told me that not only could I bring Jake with me to work for as long as I wanted, I could transform my office into a nursery. I typically shared an office, but they'd move my co-worker into a different space. In addition, a member of our Board of Directors had offered to make curtains to hang in the window separating my office from the conference room, which would allow me more privacy. I could store diapers and extra onesies and baby toys in an empty drawer. I told my boss I was worried about what would happen if Jake cried, or fussed, or whined. He seemed undaunted.

I couldn't argue that it sounded perfect. And as if to add icing to an already delectable sundae, while we sat there, a woman strolled by, a friend of my boss, the mother of twin school-aged girls. Aware of my tentative feelings about motherhood, my boss introduced this woman as a perfect example of a mother who was doing it all. She worked, raised her girls, lived in a charming downtown bungalow, played competitive softball to stay fit, and gosh dang it, she was also planning a girls-only trip for the upcoming weekend!

In fact, she did appear happy. And she was very beautiful and thin, with long red hair and flawless make-up. But I couldn't help noticing that the conversation happened entirely from a male point of view. My boss did the talking. She just sort of shrugged and agreed with his long list of compliments, and gave one-word answers to his questions. And although she didn't refute him, she also didn't encourage me. I don't think she knew what to say, and I wanted to know what she was really feeling, deep down. It had become obvious to me over the years that I'm good at wearing a mask, and I wondered if she was, too. What emotions lay under her perfectly applied foundation? Did her mascara ever run because she was stuffed into the corner of her bedroom, crying? Unfortunately, I never got the chance to ask her, which was almost worse than knowing the truth, because if she was wearing a mask, at least I'd know that, and if she wasn't, then I could expect quite a lot from myself. The unknown festered inside me.

When it came time to return to work, despite the pit in my stomach that now replaced the baby, taking up enough space to fill my entire abdomen, I forced myself to summon gratitude and shove my reservations into a dark corner. Other women I knew were putting their babies in daycare as early as six weeks, feeling torn open about handing their newborn to a stranger. And although I very much see the benefits of daycare and am a huge supporter, I wasn't ready to separate from Jake at that point.

———

Behind me, in the backseat, the engine still humming, I hear Jake waking quietly, gurgling, and I turn around and say, "Hey there," wiping tears from my cheeks. In this moment, he looks so wonderfully, perfectly, innocent, with his big blue eyes and wisps of hair, incapable of causing any conflict, and I smile, embracing the moment. I get out of the car and wind the Moby wrap around my body several times in a way that is far less graceful than the how-to guide that came inside the package; another item I didn't have before Jake was born. But after Chris and I discovered Jake's need to be held close, a friend (the same sage who brought over the swing) suggested it. The Moby Wrap essentially turns me into a walking swaddle, and Jake loves it. I know that "wearing him" is my best chance of succeeding with him in my office.

I head over to Jake's car seat and wiggle him into the wrap, pulling and tugging at the fabric until he's in a somewhat prone position. By the time I'm finished, sweat pours down my forehead. The fabric pulls uncomfortably over the left side of my neck, and I take a minute to move it, but it doesn't budge and I just leave it. So what if it tugs at my neck? I look down at Jake, and he stares back at me, content. "Love you, Sweet Thing," I say, reaching my thumb into the wrap and feeling his tiny fingers wrap around mine, swaddling me in sweetness. I swear he smiles, and this makes my heart do about three backwards flips.

I walk toward my office, holding a bag in each hand, and a baby on my front, swinging my arms, because maybe I can trick myself into feeling competent. But instead I find myself thinking about everything I'm nervous about. I feel stressed every time I'm required to do something new with Jake, and working in an office with a baby feels *new*. I go through the list I've contemplated a million times in seven weeks. My boss is male. How will I breastfeed discreetly in front of him? I respect that there are myriad ways to approach this topic, but I can say for absolute sure that I'm not the type of woman who feels comfortable breastfeeding openly in public, my breast on display to the world. I tried to practice discreet breastfeeding at home, stuffing Jake under a nursing cover, but he flailed and kicked the cover off, and his face got red because it was too hot. And then, what about sleeping? Right now Jake sleeps exclusively in his swing, in his swaddle, to the hum of the window air conditioner. I did have Chris drop off a second swing at my office—something I picked up at a used baby gear store—but how will Jake adjust to napping in an office environment that's full of talking people and ringing phones? And what about my ability to focus? How will I do both jobs, mothering and checking items off my To Do list effectively, at the same time?

When I get into my office, my boss greets me with a hug, as do all of my co-workers. They peek inside my wrap at Jake, comment on how handsome he is, and ask me a few questions about his birth. And then it's go time. I waddle into my office and set down my bags, mentally thinking about how I want to arrange things. The curtains are already hung, and in fact they look pretty and do offer privacy. Jake still seems content in the wrap, so I keep him in there while I empty the contents of the diaper bag, place things in drawers, turn on my computer, and take a quick glance at my To Do list, compiled before I left for maternity leave, and that is ten items long.

Fifteen minutes later, my boss wanders in casually, pulls up a chair and asks if I want to catch up on some work stuff. I look up. "Let's do this," I say, too cheerily.

I sit down, Jake still attached to my chest, and my boss starts catching me up. But before our conversation really even begins, I can feel Jake rooting for my nipple, a sign that he's hungry. I look at the clock. *Has it been that long?* I fed him just before I left the house to buy myself as much time as possible, but it's already been a couple of hours. It took that long to get here and get started.

My boss continues talking, and I attempt to listen intently as I mentally freak out about checking the first big stressor off my list: Nursing Baby in Front of Male Boss. But I feign confidence. Nodding and answering his questions, I pop Jake out of the Moby wrap, stand up, and move Jake from arm to arm as I unwind the wrap from my body. The fabric gets caught around my neck, and I stumble as I step on the cloth, choking myself, but smiling in a "No biggie, this happens all the time" kind of way. I release the choking sensation, cradling Jake in a position that supports his neck. My boss keeps talking, his eyes following my movements, looking sort of amused at my clunky routine.

I sigh and sit back down. *Okay.* Time to nurse. With a deep breath, I continue to hold up my end of the conversation, barely, while simultaneously placing the nursing cover over my shoulder, opening the flap on my nursing shirt, and unhooking the latch on my nursing bra. With my other hand, I place Jake under the cover. He roots around, unable to find my nipple in the midst of all that fabric, and frankly, I don't really know where it is, either. I nod at my boss (no hands available to put up my finger), tell him, "Just a minute," and look under the cover at Jake, who is becoming red-faced with impatience and heat. I move his head to my nipple, while my boss sits silently, looking around the room, trying to give me "space." Jake latches on. *Hallelujah.* All is right with the world. This office/nursery situation is okay!

And then the worst happens. Just as I've re-entered the conversation with my boss, and I can feel myself beginning to talk intelligently about an upcoming fundraising event we need to plan, remembering the details and tasks at hand, knowing just what I need to do, Jake begins to kick his legs, and then he flips his arm into the air, a dramatic movement that whips the nursing cover into the air, exposing my son's head, and my nipple, to my boss.

"Oh, no!" I say. Horrified, I stand up and turn around. But this quick movement forces Jake to detach from my breast, and he is not ready, so he begins to scream. He spits milk all over my nursing shirt and skirt, some dripping onto the floor, and he cries an octave higher than I've ever heard. He flails and wails, and I quickly cover my breast, hold him close and swing him side to side, scanning the room wildly for his pacifier.

My boss stands up. "I'll just give you some time," he says.

I nod. "Thanks."

And then I add, "This should just take a minute."

On the way out of my office, my boss turns to me. "Just relax," he says, smiling. "You'll get it." I know his intentions are pure, and he means to be encouraging, but in this moment, I want to tie the Moby Wrap around his neck and strangle him.

Jake continues to wail—I can't get him to stop, or to nurse, or to do anything but cry, and I can't find his pacifier, *fuck, did I forget it?*—and I begin to feel guilty and embarrassed about all of this commotion, so I decide to go outside to give my co-workers a break. Unable to fathom tying the Moby Wrap back on in this chaos, I cradle Jake in my bare arms and take him outside. On my way out, I pull my shirt down over my belly, and adjust my skirt up. My clothing had crept out of place in the fray, exposing my flesh almost all the way down to my C-section scar, the stitches only recently dissolved. I can feel my co-workers' eyes following me, and I can't help but feel self-conscious. My sense is that they're sending good vibes my way. But what if they're already questioning this arrangement? What if they expected me to be much more competent? The only thing that's apparent is that I'm failing miserably in my quest to have it all.

And that's when it happens. The crevasse. I'm less than fifty steps away from the front door of my office, in the side parking lot designated for the executive director and other people with paid permits, and I trip over a crack in the asphalt. It happens so fast it doesn't seem real. In a matter of two seconds, I stumble, come down hard on my right knee, and reach my arms over Jake and toward the ground to protect him. But as much as I desperately try to envelop Jake *and* break our fall, I can't do both well. He rolls out of my arms and onto the hot pavement. Horrified, on my hand and knees, I reach for him. "Jake," I say, pulling him toward me. It's like the dream where he's lost in the sheets, except much worse, because it's real and we're on a hard surface. He wails, his face an unnatural deep red. "Oh my gosh, I'm so sorry," I say. "Love, I'm sorry." I turn him over, checking for cuts, burns, or broken bones. In my mind, I've come close to killing him. I'm sure "dropping your baby on hot pavement" isn't anywhere in the brochures listing "50 Ways Your Baby Might Die," yet I've managed to do just that. Make this #51.

Jake is somehow unscathed, and I hold him to my chest. Tears stream down my cheeks. Feeling suddenly aware of this painfully public location, my incompetence on display to the world, I look around, sure that someone has called 911 or child protective services, and officials are on their way with handcuffs. But magically, thankfully there's no one around. Nobody's around to scold me or haul me away. Or help. So I sit there, the pavement burning under my butt, in what feels like an enormous pit. I hold my baby in my arms, checking him again and again for cuts or bruises, still sure that I've nearly killed him, ready to make a pact with the devil if necessary. And then I look up at the too-blue sky and at the town center that visitors describe as a "Happy Place," and I think, *I am the worst mother. I don't deserve this baby. I was right to be afraid during graduate school. Maybe that fear was a warning.*

I feel defeated, lower than I've ever been in my life. Certainly I'm not a woman who's cut out to have it all. I deserve to be deported from this country of Motherhood.

I have never fallen into a crevasse in the outdoors. But it remains, to this day, one of my greatest fears. There are stories, terrible accounts. One that stands out is about a couple of brothers who were traversing a series of canyons in Utah. Due to an error with their rope length, one of them fell into a deep canyon, out of sight, seriously wounded. His brother could hear him, but not reach him. For hours, he listened to his brother's fruitless calls and whimpers. Eventually, he had to leave. He had to let his brother die alone.

In my own crevasse, which is a stupid tiny crack in the

cement, I sit. Of course I can stand up and step out. But when I look down, I see that my knee is bleeding, evidence of my fall, something I will have to explain to my co-workers, and Chris. And interestingly, a feeling of relief washes over me. It will be a way to describe what's happening to me, proof of my raw state. I hope someone can not only hear me, but help.

5

Fantasies Aren't Real

Three Months into Motherhood

I lie in a bunk bed in a canvas yurt in the middle of the woods. It's Saturday morning, silent, except for the crackling of fire in the wood stove and the chirping of birds outside. Next to me, Chris is sprawled out on his back, snoring. Jake's asleep in his baby swing in the middle of the room. His head rests on his chest, cheeks puffed out over his chin, legs dangling. Through the frosted dome on the vaulted ceiling, I watch the hazy light of dawn. Soft rays creep down, finger-like, touching the table, wood bin and frying pan.

This is the fantasy I fell in love with when I was pregnant, the one I promised myself I'd make real. And it's happening—Chris and me in the wilderness with our new baby, the three of us flowing with the natural rhythms of the outdoors. There are trees and trails, camp fires and cabins, wildlife, stars and silence. From the outside, it looks idyllic.

Jake squeals. My left breast shoots needle-like pain and my shoulders tense. His face scrunches up and he makes fists with his hands and the whole room fills with his wails. Wall-to-wall cries. In one second flat, the yurt transforms from a peaceful room to a place that's vibrating with urgent need. In my chest it feels like an earthquake. "Ouch," I say, rolling to my side.

My fingers move from my C-section scar to the top of my T-shirt, which is wet from leaked milk, both breasts painfully engorged. My body, from neck to upper thighs—the entire core—still feels squishy and broken, unable to support the muscles of my arms and legs. It takes all of my effort just to push up to a sitting position.

Jake's shrieks get louder, and my pulse rockets, my throat tightens and my brain fires maternal alarms. "Panic," it shouts, "Panic!" Next to me, Chris stirs only slightly in his sleep. Overwhelmed, I just sit there looking around the room, trembling. I know what to do, or at least I should. The minute that umbilical cord was cut, I magically transformed into a capable mother. Right? I still question this every day.

We've been here for three days, at this yurt in the Colorado Forest. It's our first getaway with Jake, the result of the epiphany I had in Walmart, when I decided to find ways, small and big, to keep me feeling whole; a last-ditch attempt to dig myself out of my own crevasse, because in fact, no one has heard my calls. I've simply continued stumbling and standing back up.

Before Jake was born, Chris and I would've classified this type of trip as Easy, a total no-brainer, because we were able to drive right up to the yurt with all of our belongings. This time, that meant bringing the baby swing (i.e. still our son's bed), a bouncy chair, a pile of blankets, various swaddles and sleepers, and four pacifiers, which is overkill, but Jake is a pacifier junkie and although Team: Self Soothing in the Mommy Wars would tell us this means now our kid won't be able to calm himself without assistance until he's like fifteen years old, or maybe never, and possibly it will mean he'll become a co-dependent addict (there are stats to support anything), neither Chris nor I give a shit. We're surviving with pacifiers and they get lost all the time, bouncing and rolling and disappearing worse than silly putty. (We still haven't figured out how to clasp the pacifier to Jake's shirt. The rope didn't work. But someone did introduce us recently to a "pacifier leash," which has been added to the We Need list.) We're bringing a ton of stuff, because after baby, this trip feels big. At the moment, it feels enormous.

Chris did not think this trip was a good idea. When I mentioned it, I was sprawled out on the bed one evening, exhausted after a day at my office/nursery, and I could hear more than a hint of desperation in my voice. I needed a positive response and hoped Chris's eyes would light up with enthusiasm and that he'd turn on his heel, pick up his phone and make a reservation. Even more, I wish he'd been the one to suggest the trip, wishing himself for the adventure.

But when I said, "Hey, how about a yurt trip?" Chris looked at me, bit his lower lip, and then began to do something that would become his own troubling trademark, a parallel pattern to my need to do it all. He began to make The List. Not a list of everything we should pack, but of why we shouldn't go. For starters, he wondered if it was safe to take a newborn baby to 9,000 feet elevation. We wouldn't have any access to medical services. And where would Jake sleep in a yurt? Would it be warm enough? And then, there were wild animals: Coyotes and bears and mountain lions. Do coyotes steal babies? And holy shit, how many diapers would we have to pack? Was it possible to calculate the need?

I flipped over on my stomach and glared at him. "What about our adventure list!" I yelled. I glanced over toward where I knew the list was, on the bookshelf, tucked into my journal. At the moment, it was buried under the pile of brochures from the hospital, and it would practically take an archaeology expedition to uncover it, but it was there. I knew that. And I still thought of it often when I traversed the bedroom from my nursing chair to the bed. "Chris, remember what we promised?" I asked.

Chris looked at me, unblinking. "Carrie, we have to be realistic."

I thought back to when we agreed to spend our lives together, when I was high on the notion that two people like us—an adventurer and a homebody—could be a perfect balance for each other, yet I wondered, deep down, how it would work in real life. Things are easy for the first few miles, but then what? We were at that point.

"I am being realistic," I said.

Chris shrugged. "Fine, I'll call the pediatrician and see what she says."

It was our own private version of the Mommy Wars, happening in the battleground of our bedroom. *Parents, start your engines.*

Chris left the room. I buried my head in my hands. It's not that I didn't wonder the same things. I was unsure about a yurt trip, too, but I didn't want to be told no. Also, I was still immersed in genetics—checking Jake daily for signs of disorders that wouldn't necessarily have been apparent at birth like cystic fibrosis and Fragile X Syndrome. *Was Jake making eye contact? Smiling? Was the frequency and color of his poop normal? Did he eat enough?* And SIDS was an ongoing threat. I was making myself crazy and needed a getaway to get away from my own brain. Our house was too full of feeding charts and poop logs and newborn brochures and manuals, and the "50 Ways Your Baby Might Die." They kept reminding me, in their bold letters, to watch for this, and this, and this. I needed a change of scenery, a reset.

Our pediatrician gave Chris great news. She said to go. (At least it was good news for me. Inside, I gave myself a high five and added a sponsor logo to my racecar.) She had no qualms about our trip, and she said the only thing to note is that Jake would probably nurse more frequently. Traveling from 5,000 to 9,000 feet elevation means thinner air, requiring more fluid intake. Chris and I knew about this from our pre-baby backcountry trips—we always prepared to drink double our normal amount.

And it's true–on this trip, Jake has been feeding every two or three hours all day and night, which has signaled my body to produce more milk. Biologically, I find this fascinating—how a woman's body adjusts and implements immediate changes to meet the baby's needs. But in reality, it meant that my body was out of the rhythm we'd established, and my breasts seemed to be reprimanding me.

In the thunderstorm of Jake's cries, I stall. I wait for something—for what? For Chris to wake up, pick Jake up, and hand him to me to do my job? I don't feel ready to go to "work." I want a day off. Now, several weeks back at my nonprofit job, I think America's typical maternity leave policies are even more ludicrous than I did on the day I re-entered the office. A few weeks or months of motherhood is enough time to get used to, approximately, nothing. Despite being offered the perfect return-to-work situation, and being grateful for that, the main thing I feel is this: Instead of doing one challenging job, I am doing two at the same time, managing Jake's schedule in my office-nursery, as well as meetings and phone calls and planning a major fundraising event. The added demands only escalated my anxiety. Instead of feeling like a whole person, I felt fragmented. My core identity was lost in the fray, rendering me powerless. It made me question: Did I really like my job? Did I even care about it? How did I want to spend my time? What was important to me in life?

With a desperation that rocks me, I want Jake's cries to stop, yet I don't have the energy to stop them. "Hey," I say, elbowing Chris in the side.

He half-opens his eyes and then springs up. "Oh," he says, immediately awake. "Sorry, I didn't hear him. Let me get him this time."

He crawls over me, his bare feet slapping the floor. Jake's cries slow but don't stop when Chris cuddles him. I prop myself up on some pillows, and it's only when Jake is in my arms and latched on to my breast that he finally calms. *I do know what to do,* I think. A tiny thread of relief travels through me.

Chris stokes the fire and gets the coffee pot going and takes a peek out the door. "Gorgeous morning," he says.

Jake sucks ravenously, his face pink and stern, and slowly,

slowly, the pressure in my breasts eases. He looks up at me with big wet blue eyes and I stroke his bald head and think I've never seen a more beautiful child in my life. "I love you," I say, and wonder why I can't always feel the peace I do in this moment. Why do Jake's cries throw me into such a panic? Why do I sleep so lightly, if at all, even when Jake's fast asleep?

Chris crawls back into bed. He hands me a packet of M&M's. I smile. "Chocolate for breakfast. My favorite."

He pops an M&M into his mouth and takes a long, deep breath. "This is so nice," he says. "Relaxing."

I nod and half-smile, chomping on my chocolate, moving Jake to the other breast. Chris snuggles in next to me and rubs my arm, and then moves his hand toward my free breast. I gently push him away.

"Sorry," he says.

"No, it's not you," I touch his arm. "It's just…" How do I explain to my husband that all of this touching makes me want to explode? Especially when Jake is attached to my breast, I can't handle another human. My breasts used to evoke sensual feelings for both Chris and me, but now they're double D's, and although I often catch Chris staring at them hungrily, to me they feel like big sloppy sacks of milk. When he reaches to touch me, I want to slice off his hand with an ax. I long to feel sexy again, for me, and I want to meet Chris's needs, and to reconnect as a couple. It seems like this should be happening by now, but it's not.

"It's okay," says Chris, moving back a few inches. "Did you get any sleep last night?"

I shrug. "A little."

He glances up at my eyes. "You look really tired."

I look away.

I can tell he so badly wants to touch me, to comfort me.

He sighs. "Carrie, I think you should try the meds."

I look at him, startled. "What?"

"You know, the meds that the midwife recommended."

I think about our midwife, her comments about postpartum depression. "She didn't 'recommend' anything," I snap.

"Okay, 'suggested.'"

"I don't remember her *suggesting* anything, either."

He bites his bottom lip.

I turn toward him. "Why are you bringing this up?" I ask.

Chris sighs. "Carrie, you have to admit, you're just not yourself. Here we are in the middle of the woods, where you usually feel most alive and relaxed, and you *still* can't sleep."

I tense up, defensive. My mind shoots the same cycle of thoughts forward. *I am a strong woman. I have a healthy baby and a helpful husband. I am not a failure. Why is he telling me I'm a failure?*

But when I look into Chris' eyes, I only see love and honesty and genuine concern for my well-being. Deep down, I know he's right. It makes me think back to when my genetics professor pulled me into her office for that candid conversation, or when I fell into the crack in the asphalt outside my nonprofit office. Both times, I was hoping someone would hear me calling. Well, this time it's Chris. He's heard me, and he's reaching his rope down to pull me out. It's my choice to grab on or not.

"I don't know what's wrong with me," I whisper. "Why can't I do this? Why is this so hard?"

"Sweetheart." He sits up. "It is hard. It's hard for me, too. But some of this stuff—the sleep stuff and depression—it's out of your control. It's the pregnancy and hormones. Didn't you hear the midwife? She said postpartum depression affects a lot of women."

In fact, I'd barely heard the midwife. She'd also heard my call, but I'd tuned her out. I was too focused on my fantasy, refusing to accept that a baby might change my life in even small ways, that pregnancy might deeply alter my body chemistry, that the adjustment to motherhood might be bigger than anything I'd ever known, rocking my world. I didn't even entertain what that might look like. Yet I know fantasies aren't real.

At our last appointment, my midwife insisted on going through the symptoms of postpartum depression, one by one, with me: trouble sleeping, anxiety, depressed mood. I was experiencing all of those things, in surround sound. So why do I continue to insist postpartum depression is not me? Why am I intent on doing it all—working and mothering and connecting with my husband and exercising and cooking and cleaning—all at the same time? Why do I think something's wrong with me?

The reality is that I don't know anyone who's happily doing it all. My peers who are moms are all struggling for balance, trying to figure out who they are, and often questioning their choice to work, or not work, or somewhere in between. As for celebrities who pretend to be doing it all perfectly, I believe they're lying. Or superhuman. Or in some cases, they're superrich.

Chris reads my mind. "Besides the meds, I think we need to work out ways for you to have breaks, because you need time by yourself. Not just time to work at your office, but to write, because you love that, and to be alone."

The thought of this—writing in my journal, doing anything alone—releases a well of emotion that squeezes my chest.

We sit in silence for a few minutes, and I place my hand in his. I ponder his words.

"So, hey," says Chris cheerfully, propping himself up on his elbow. "Let's start now. When you're done feeding Jake, why don't you go out for a walk?"

I smile. His compassion and enthusiasm make him so special. Maybe he resisted this trip, and that annoyed me, but he knows me well. He knows that even in my state of severe sleep deprivation and discomfort, the thought of a solo walk in the woods makes my heart leap. I look over at my hiking clothes, which are in a pile on the adjacent bunk bed, next to my backpack and my almost-blank journal.

"Okay," I say.

"Good," says Chris. "That's decided." He flops on his back.

"But when I'm gone you'll make sure to burp Jake, right?" I ask. "There are a stack of burp cloths…"

"Yes," Chris interrupts. "I'll burp him."

"And after you burp him, he can't be on his tummy for a while, and then…"

"Stop," says Chris. He looks annoyed.

"Sorry."

His face is stern. "I can certainly take care of Jake while you're gone for an hour."

I nod eagerly.

And I do know. I guess I'm projecting my own insecurities onto him. In reality, Chris is just as competent as I am—we're both figuring parenthood out—and I need to trust him to do things his own way.

I touch his cheek. "Thank you for knowing me," I say, and I mean this on many levels.

He rolls toward me and touches my lips. "I love you," he says. "I love you too." I wipe my tears with his thumb.

In the forest, I take everything slowly. I roll my shoulders and twist my hips and pause to prick my thumb with a pine needle. I notice that the long meadow grass tickles my ankles, and I breathe deeply, the scent of pine and earth filling my nose. A pair of squirrels frolics nearby, chasing each other through the trees and bushes, and I pick up my pace, trying to catch them. My muscles begin to feel long and loose, and I fall into a rhythm—one foot in front of the other, spine straight, arms swinging; a posture that is wholly my own. *My body.*

Out here, with no walls or windows or external demands, my vision clears. I can see that this trip—this foray into the high altitude forest with my brand new family—has actually been a great success. Except for eating more frequently, Jake has seemed perfectly at home in our new surroundings. He's hiked with us in the Moby Wrap, slept in his swing, and gurgled as I read him a book in front of the fire. It makes me wonder: Why *am* I so hard on myself?

I think of my childhood, my upbringing with self-sufficient, strong-willed, and stubborn parents. Besides raising kids, my parents did every domestic task themselves. They cleaned the house, washed the car, mowed the lawn, painted the walls, trimmed the bushes, changed the oil in the Oldsmobile, and when it came time to move, they packed everything themselves. Not that we could afford domestic help—we lived on my dad's high school teaching salary—but I had the sense, even then, that this wasn't only about money. My parents were committed to hard work, and I learned to be independent and strong, that success needed to be earned, within the four walls of the little one-story house in which they raised me. Plus, it ran even deeper. I'd inherited their DNA, right?

But maybe I've become so consumed with strength and independence that I'm not able to ask for help–at all. Maybe I need, instead, to focus on being resourceful.

At an intersection, I have the choice to walk up a steep hill or continue on the flat path. I choose the hill and break into a full sweat as I listen to my hiking boots thumping against rock. *Ba-rump. Ba-rump.* My thighs and calves tremble and it feels good, this exertion, because I am alone, in my body, having a miniature solo adventure while my husband takes care of our child. Slightly, just slightly, I notice something striking: There are muscles firing deep in my abdomen, my core, the center of my physical strength, and also the home of my true identity. I thought it was dead, starting during my C-section, when I was conscious yet unable to feel the surgeon slice open my flesh and hold my internal organs in the air, continuing with this depression and feeling like a stranger in my own completely changed body. But my core is alive. It's barely breathing, but it's there. I try lifting my right leg up over a tree stump—the leg that's been lagging in strength, that I've been unable to lift over my bike frame—and it raises a couple inches higher than ever before. I feel triumphant. It's similar to the feeling I had in Germany, when things began clicking.

After ten minutes of hard climbing, I take a break, breathing fast. I wipe sweat off my brow and look around, wondering what's further uphill. There's a boulder ahead, and I climb up to get a better view. But when I put my fingers into a crevice and heave, my body doesn't move. My arms are not strong enough. My entire chest aches.

"Damn," I say, to an Aspen tree. I rest my head on the trunk. I taste the bark with my tongue.

And then, in one smooth motion, I wrap my arms around the tree. I hold the trunk and hoist myself up the boulder, the gray wood arching deeply to support my weight, and I scramble up, and up more. On top, I beam.

"Thank you, tree," I say.

As I crane my neck to see the mountain peaks in the distance through the trees, I think about how this moment mirrors my journey. And I make a promise, a brand new one. I hold my hands in the air and commit to let go of my fantasy and begin to create my reality. I say this out loud to the trees and the squirrels and the peak in the distance.

"I will let go," I say, "And move on."

Which makes me realize something interesting: *Motherhood* has elicited this moment of illumination. It's what has torn me down, pushed me off center, and ripped my core to shreds. But this, in turn, has forced me into a place of authenticity where I'm committed to identifying my life's top priorities. Maybe the wrapping paper is unseemly, but it's a pretty big gift. I pull my journal out of my pocket and write all of this down, because I know it will keep me accountable to make a change. I record the date and time and place and jot down some notes. With that, I jump down from the boulder and begin my descent to the yurt, holding my journal tight in my hands.

6

Un-Adventure

Nine Months into Motherhood

The sun is hot on my chest. Not because I'm lying on a warm boulder in the wilderness or reclining next to a babbling river in my bikini. We're in the Denver airport—Chris, Jake, and me—our chairs facing the expansive floor-to-ceiling windows, and the morning sun reflects off the snow, bursting with heat. As we wait for our late plane to arrive at the gate and whisk us away, I try to pretend we're already there. Sand, margaritas, seashells. Florida. *Our big, fluffy, un-adventure.*

Jake fidgets in my lap. "Ba!" he screams. "Boo." He pushes to stand on his skinny legs and wobbles around on my thighs.

"Hey, honey, shhh," I say, touching his butter-soft cheek. He lunges forward, lips glistening with drool from teething, and a strand of spit lands on my face. "Thanks, bud," I say, wiping it away. He beams a big, cheesy grin, and I can't help but laugh. "You goof," I say. As we lock eyes, I think my heart might burst with a giant cliché of love.

"Ma ma," says Jake, and I melt further. I notice that his

eyes are watery—the first sign he's getting sleepy—and then he reaches up a hand and rubs them.

"Oh, boy," I whisper, glancing over at the customer service counter. I squint to see the departure time. It still says 8:55, the original time, even though my cell phone reads 8:57, and the runway in front of us is deserted. "Come on," I say, glaring at an employee in a smooth uniform with smooth hair. I brush my fingers through my own (stringy) hair and try to communicate with her telepathically. *Let's get this show on the road. Don't you see I have a baby here? He needs to nap and we have to change planes in Chicago. Chicago! We cannot miss our connection.*

I consider O'Hare the worst airport in the country, because I missed my grandmother's funeral when I was in college, stuck there for twelve hours, sitting on the shiny, coffin-like floor. I handled it as calmly as I could—the power was out of my hands—but would rather not repeat that experience today. Although we're not going anywhere nearly as important, we do have a baby. When I was browsing ticket options, I scrutinized each and every itinerary. O'Hare was non-negotiable, but everything else about this schedule seemed to be perfect. If the plane left at 9 a.m., Jake could nap at his normal time, eat some applesauce at the end of the flight—layover, plane change—and then he'd be ready for his second nap. Voila! He'd wake up, snack on some puffs, and we'd be in the van heading to our hotel, just in time for his 7 p.m. bedtime. The perfection of the timing made the idea of our first flight with Jake seem almost easy.

Except my plans are already shot. Even if the plane arrived right this minute, we wouldn't leave for another half hour, or more, throwing everything off schedule enough to make a difference. I realize this isn't a *real* problem, not in the context of real-world problems, and I'm embarrassed that I feel this way. But I can't help it. I'm anxious. I glare harder at the employee in the smooth suit, my eyes steel and unwavering, but she doesn't look back. She just shifts paper around on her counter, randomly typing something on her computer, picking up the phone and laughing, like everything is fine in the world.

"God," I say to Chris, who is reading a spy novel. I point to the counter. "Do you see her? Shouldn't she be making an announcement? Or some actually serious phone calls?"

Chris looks over. "It's no skin off her nose."

"Well, it should be," I snap.

He shrugs. "Maybe they can make up time in the air." Chris used to travel for work, so he's not fazed by delays. And typically I'm not, either. On past trips to Europe, I've navigated multiple plane changes without breaking stride. But this parenthood thing—it frazzles me *out*. We've begun to feel relatively comfortable hiking and camping with Jake in the wilderness, when the schedule is in our control and space is wide open, but air travel is different. It evokes my greatest insecurities. What if I can't get Jake to nap on the plane? How will I change his diaper if he poops? What if he cries and I can't console him and everyone on the plane is staring at me, completely pissed off?

It all seems to come down to what I can or cannot do, stuff that I still haven't mastered in the comfort of our house, partly because things are always changing. Every month brings something new. If I'm baffled half the time there, how I am going to handle these tasks in a two-foot-wide leather seat with people all around me?

Luckily, Chris is on the same internal parenthood clock as I am, so we're in this together. He knows just as well as I do that it's time for Jake's nap. We've both seen our son when he's sleep deprived, and it's a fussy, whiny, monstrous situation that we like to avoid at all costs.

"Here, you want me to hold him?" Chris asks. He puts down his book, holds out his arms, and Jake springs over. "I'll walk him around, try to get him to sleep." He stands up and flips Jake onto his shoulder. I cringe. It's not at all how I would hold Jake, especially if I were trying to put him to sleep, but I bite my tongue, refusing to micro-manage. *Freedom*, I think. *He can do it his way, and I get freedom.*

"Thanks," I say. I stand up, place our carry-on on the seat, stretch my arms over my head, and pace back and forth along the window, willing our aircraft to arrive. I look up into the abysmal depths of the blue sky. *Come on, airplane*, I think, *land*. Another family—parents with two kids—looks over at me sympathetically. They have three carry-ons, a car seat, and a stroller bursting with blankets and sun hats and diapers and fruit snacks. A lone pink flip flop sits under their chair. Although their younger child, a kid about Jake's age, is asleep in his mom's arms, their toddler is wildly galloping across the floor, making loud, annoying horse noises.

"Annabelle," the dad shouts. "Get back here." She totally ignores him.

I've been calling this trip to Florida an "un-adventure" because we're doing everything we would've never done before having a kid. Like staying in a hotel that, according to their website, is "a block from the beach," with a pool and restaurant, and a person who will meet us at the airport and transport us in a van directly to our room, which will be attached to another room, and another, which is probably next to the ice machine, or a vending machine, or some other glowing/buzzing device.

Most people would consider it paradise. Pretty much everyone I told used that exact word, eyes wide with jealousy. *You're going to Florida*, they said? *That sounds like paradise.* But my idea of utopia is different, for some reason. It makes me uncomfortable when people do stuff for me that I could easily do myself, like find my way to ground transportation, or carry luggage. It's my childhood again, creeping in. I like to go places not everyone else goes, even though it requires extra effort. I travel to get out of my comfort zone, not to simply move my comfort zone to a new location.

And I know I'm not alone. My friend in Montana, another adventurous spirit, says her biggest challenge in parenting is her constant lust for more; the eternal conflict of wanting something for you, but wanting your children too, and doing the right thing. She loves to whitewater kayak, but her kids are too young for the wild stuff like Class IV rapids. So she compromises, opting for slower paddles, and the hardest part has been wanting more adventure, but feeling selfish for that and thinking she should compromise more, and then feeling guilty for that. Always, a quandary.

In our case, Chris and I are doing this trip to Florida because it's been an especially cold winter in Colorado, and Florida is a place in the U.S. that seems predictably sunny *and* warm in February. And I found a stellar deal on a hotel.

Oh, and major development: I just quit my nonprofit job. I

got a check for my unused vacation time, so Chris and I split the money—half to Jake's education fund, half to our travel fund, and we decided this trip would be a good way to hit the "reset" button.

I quit my job because after several months of trying with everything I had to embrace my office/nursery, giving my perfect work situation the best possible chance for success, trying to find peace with "having it all," one of my colleagues told me I wasn't fun anymore now that I had a baby. He sipped his coffee and said, "Carrie, you used to be so relaxed. You used to laugh easily. Now you always seem so rushed and stressed. You're a different person."

I was speechless and irate. *Of course I was a different person! Did he not see this infant attached to my hip while I typed emails? Didn't he watch me get up and leave meetings because Jake was fussing? How lighthearted would he feel if he had a baby suckling his breast while talking to a client on the phone and attempting to keep a nursing cover in place?*

At the same time, I had to admit he was right. I didn't feel fun. Or lighthearted. I felt trapped. I did not have it all, because *I* was missing. Maybe my colleague's approach to sharing this information was crude, but I believed his intentions were pure and I appreciated his candor. I wanted myself back, too, and I'd been pondering the promise I made to myself on that boulder in the wilderness near the yurt—my pact to let go of my fantasy and create my new reality. My life had changed—that was obvious.

Recently, I'd begun taking anti-depressants. Finally, I'd accepted help. At the urging of my midwife (again), I read through the clinical signs of postpartum depression and acknowledged that the condition does not necessarily mean you're on the verge of killing your baby. It also doesn't mean you cry every second of every day, a complete basket case unable to function. In my case, I'd occasionally have pretty good days, feeling like all was relatively okay. But then the next day, I'd plummet again. My midwife convinced me that this had nothing to do with strength and competence and helpful husbands–it was about a chemical imbalance. The levels of the neurotransmitters serotonin and dopamine in my body were out of balance. I'd studied biochemistry, so why couldn't I understand this? I could. Sort of. It would've been much more palatable if we were talking about someone else, someone who wasn't as independent and self-sufficient, with a helpful husband and a healthy baby.

While I wasn't convinced that I'd have spiraled so low if my imminent return to work hadn't been hanging over my head—I wondered how situational my depression was and again considered maternity leave policies—I'd never know for sure. There would never be concrete scientific evidence, and it didn't really matter. I accepted my reality. But I pushed back as much as possible, taking the lowest dose of medication as humanly possible, cutting the minuscule pills from the pharmacy in half with a butcher knife, a surgery that proved I was still the physician in charge.

It takes time for the medication to work—several weeks—and although I wasn't feeling an immediate significant change in my mood, the act of accepting help brought new clarity. The decision had the opposite effect of what I anticipated. Instead of making me feel like a failure, it gave me strength, and it enabled me to take another step I knew was necessary: Accepting help with childcare. Two mornings a week, Chris's parents came over to babysit Jake. It was a situation that was good for everyone because they were happy to spend time with their grandson, and I got to work in a baby free (i.e. sane!) environment. Doing one job at once was so much better than two. In addition, Chris and I were exploring affordable daycare options outside the home, because we felt that Jake was getting to an age where he'd enjoy socializing with other kids.

All of this opened me up to addressing the serious questions I'd written about in my journal that needed action: What *did* I want to do with my time? As much as I wished it to, my nonprofit job didn't feel fulfilling anymore. Writing-wise, I'd been getting more freelance assignments and I'd been accepted into the professional science organization that I'd been hoping for, which made me feel sort of full-circle about my education, and that was satisfying. The work provided a little bit of income, too. But was it enough? I brainstormed all over my journal and decided I wanted to take yet another leap. I wanted to embrace these opportunities I'd been given to write professionally because I could use my creativity and contribute to society in a way that felt meaningful to me. Also, it would allow me more time to be a present mother and wife and friend, and to incorporate adventure into my life. To live from my core.

Chris and I knew we'd have to make some financial choices in order to accommodate our decrease in income, but we were both up for the challenge, partly because this decision felt as necessary for my well-being—and our relationship as a couple—as my choice to leave genetic counseling. Plus, I was starting to feel accustomed to taking these kinds of leaps. It seemed that I was finally landing in the place I'd intuited back in high school: To work as a writer.

Growing up in my middle class family taught me a lot about managing money. It's a life skill that has been invaluable to me. Chris and I sat down with our list of income and expenses—the one we made when I was pregnant, in order to calculate the length of my maternity leave—and we made modifications. We were able to cross off even more expenses from our first go-round, because we were getting used to this, too. No more expensive cable TV. We didn't need a land line. Eating out would be reserved for one night a week, which would make us appreciate it more. I could certainly cut down on my wine intake. Also, we were about to pay off our auto loan, and instead of upgrading to a new car, we decided to tuck away the payment into our travel fund. Interestingly, these decisions were no longer feeling like sacrifices; rather, they were liberating. We didn't realize how much we *wouldn't miss something* until it was gone, until we saw how much freedom it brought, supporting the lifestyle we desired.

And then we did something kind of crazy. We spent a whole bunch of money. We leveraged the equity on our home in order to purchase an investment property. Immediately, this began providing some monthly cash flow, offsetting lost income, and the property would appreciate over time, providing college savings for Jake.

When I started searching for vacation rentals in Florida, I did so halfheartedly because what I really wanted was a trip to rural Mexico, even though my only experience with Mexico was in bigger cities like Mazatlan and Oaxaca, and I didn't know exactly why I wanted this, or what rural place I'd go. But I've always found Mexico to be very beautiful and affordable, sunny and warm, and in my mind, anywhere south of the border offers some layer of adventure, at the very least because I could practice my Spanish. But Jake was at the age where he was always putting stuff in his mouth, and I wondered if it would be responsible to take him to Mexico, especially to a less developed town. What if we exposed him to a dangerous insect bite or virus, or a scorpion sting? How would I live with myself if something bad happened?

Chris was thrilled when I told him I'd booked the hotel in Florida. He perused the website, noting all of the wonderful amenities. "Check out this pool!" he said. "And hey, there's a nice footpath all the way to the beach! There are chaises on the sand!" He couldn't believe the low price I'd negotiated.

"Yeah, it'll be good," I said, wishing he was less enthusiastic and hoping, like me, for a rugged trail to the beach and deserted sand.

Instead, he gave me a high five. "This is going to be amazing." When he saw me frowning, he balked. "What's wrong?"

I looked down. "I don't know."

"Would you rather be going somewhere else?"

"Yeah."

"Like where?"

"Mexico. Europe. Bali. The middle of nowhere."

He rolled his eyes. "Carrie, that's just not possible right now." He began doing it again: The List. He began listing reasons why Florida was our best choice, and the others weren't realistic— we have a baby, the flights are too long, he can't take that much time off work, there are diseases in foreign places, and on and on. I sighed. It's not that he was wrong—I didn't disagree with most of his arguments—but this pattern of communication closed off our conversations before they even started. I felt like my ideas were being trashed. It crushed possibility before I had a chance to even plant a seed.

"Whatever," I said, which had become my typical response to The List. "I feel fortunate that we can take this trip. I just wish we were going somewhere more adventurous." I walked away.

———

In the waiting area of the Denver airport, as I amble around and Chris wanders the corridors trying to get Jake to sleep, the mother with the baby looks at me. "How old is your son?" she asks.

"Nine months."

"Oh, ours is ten."

"Aw," I say. "He's cute." Really, the only thing I notice is that he's bald. I've always despised traveling on airplanes near children because I hate it when they whine, cry, kick the seat, or talk loud. Even now that I'm a parent, the one lugging a kid on the plane, I have that instinctual reaction.

"Where are you guys going?" she asks.

"Sanibel."

"Oh, us too!"

She asks where we're staying, and it's not the same place, which is a relief, because now we won't have to get together for drinks just because we both happen to have children. Her baby wakes and she pulls a nursing cover out of her purse and slips him underneath. As she fumbles around trying to get him appropriately hooked up, she glances up at me. "Are you breastfeeding?" she asks.

I shake my head. "Not anymore. I stopped a few months ago."

"Ah," she says. "I'm thinking about stopping, but I can't decide when. He's so into it."

We both giggle.

"Men," she says, and we laugh again.

There's an uncomfortable silence, so I say, "Well, I guess he'll stop when he's ready," which I realize is stupid, and possibly not even accurate, but I can't think of anything else.

She shrugs. "You're probably right. My daughter was done at six months. I've heard boys go a lot longer."

"Oh." I'd never heard anything like that.

"Man, I need this vacation," she says, suddenly. She looks deep into my eyes.

I have to admit I agree. "Yeah, me too."

We share an instant of motherly connection—suspended together in that exhausted, overwhelmed, disoriented place—and I almost ask her if she's ever dealt with postpartum depression. We'd just been talking about breastfeeding, right? And I really wanted to talk to someone. Would my anxiety ever be gone completely? Would I eventually feel less insecure? I still felt so alone. On paper, I was a statistic–one of many affected. But in real life, no one I knew was talking about it.

The woman interrupts my thoughts. "Have you been to Sanibel before?" she asks.

I shake my head. "No."

"Oh, you'll love it!" she exclaims. "It's the most amazing place. You don't have to lift a finger. The service is excellent everywhere. The hardest thing you have to do every day is walk to the beach, or the golf course." She snorts, her mind undoubtedly focused on chaise lounges and Mai Tais.

And just like that, our connection is lost. Before I can respond with real-sounding fake optimism, her baby's eyes shoot out from under the cover, and he yawns, pumping his fists in the air. I exhale, taking this as my out, my opportunity to head to the customer service counter, where I can start asking questions and maybe raise a little hell.

"Hey," she asks. "Can you hold him a second?"

My mouth opens. "What?"

"Just for a second? I have to use the restroom. And my husband, well, you can see what he's doing." She frowns.

I scan the waiting area. Her husband is trying to peel their daughter off the railing of the moving walkway. I move toward her stiffly and put my arms out like I'm about to catch a football. The child is soft and warm, and weighs about the same as Jake. He looks up at me like I'm an alien, and I really don't blame him. I bounce him around on my shoulder, so he doesn't have to see me, this strange woman who is not his mother.

"Thanks," she says. "Just two minutes." She looks over at her husband, waves to get his attention, mouths some angry-looking words, and then walks in the other direction. "I am not dealing with him," she says. "He's going to have to figure it out."

"Oh." I glance at him. He rolls his eyes and I sort of half-shrug.

As I jiggle their baby around the foot-wide space of the chair, I can't help but think about what it would be like to have two children. Chris and I have just begun to have this conversation, but I'm not ready. Right now it seems painfully out of my league. As I look back and forth between the baby I'm holding and his sister, who is now screaming, "No, Daddy" into her father's face, I shudder.

A woman speaks into a microphone. "Ladies and gentlemen," she says.

I look over at the ticket counter. It's the employee I was glaring at earlier. "Our plane has arrived at the gate," she says. I look out the window, and it's true–it's here! I practically jump out of the chair. "Yes!" I say to the baby. He gurgles. I do a little dance with him.

His mother returns, looking slightly disconcerted with the way I'm bouncing him around, and she takes him back. "Thank you," she says, patting her bladder. She waves her husband over wildly, and he shakes his head, exasperated, pointing at their daughter. She motions, one-handed, for him to pick the girl up. He throws his hands in the air. "God," she whispers to me, "Men are so incompetent."

I shift my feet uncomfortably. I try really hard not to view Chris as incompetent, because he's not. Technically, neither of us knows for sure what we're doing, and sometimes I catch myself playing the martyr just because I'm the woman, the mom, the person in the family who is supposed to be a domestic goddess.

"Well, have a nice trip," I say.

She smiles at me distractedly. "Yeah, you too."

When I turn away, I see Chris coming back. Jake is asleep in his arms. My eyes widen. *Holy shit*, I think, *he put Jake to sleep, even while holding him in that weird way.* I give him a thumbs up, trying not to look the least bit surprised.

We reunite at our carry-on, and Chris snuggles close to my side, playfully tapping my hip with his. "Just call me the baby whisperer," he says.

I smile. "Good work, babe."

He puffs out his chest. "I know you didn't think it would work."

"What do you mean?" I giggle.

He rolls his eyes. "Remember this moment forever. I put our son to sleep in the middle of an airport."

"Very funny."

"Just call me 'Dad of the Year.'"

"Ha." But I have to admit I like this. I like that Chris feels empowered.

"We're boarding soon," I say.

He looks over at the customer service counter. "Sweet," he says. "We're not even that late. Sand and sunshine, here were come."

"Yep."

He frowns. "Are you even excited about this trip?"

"Yes!"

"No, you're not."

"I am."

"Why did you even book it if you don't want to go?"

I change the subject. "Let me hold him for a while," I say, holding my arms out toward Jake. I snuggle him close to my chest and breathe in his sweet powdery scent.

By some stroke of enormous luck, Jake sleeps all the way to O'Hare. I keep looking down at him on the airplane, his mouth open in an O-shape, his breathing fast and heavy, waiting for him to wake up screaming, but he doesn't. Chris and I glance at each other every few minutes, shrugging and smiling and mouthing words of surprise. Chris orders a beer, and I order diet soda (caffeine addiction still looming). I make some notes in my journal while Chris gets happily lost in the sports channel. I feel my shoulders relax and my breath lengthen. Several rows behind us, I can hear a baby fussing, a toddler whining, and the strained voices of stressed-out parents. It's probably the family I saw in the waiting room, and I cross my fingers that Jake will sleep just a touch longer.

Upon landing at O'Hare, our luck completely runs out. Jake wakes up, and he is pissed. He opens his mouth wide, scrunches up his forehead, and his face turns beet red. It is several seconds before the sound comes out, and when it does, it's piercing, several decibels higher than the robotic squeaks of the landing gear.

Chris pulls his headphones off, a freaked out look on his face. "Whoa, buddy," he says.

I cradle Jake in my arms, rocking him fast. "Sh, sh, sh," I say.

Jake doesn't come close to stopping. I take a deep breath. *You know how to handle this. Pretend you're at home.* I turn to Chris. "Hey, can you grab—"

Chris reads my mind. He digs around in our carry-on and pulls out the pacifier. Jake lunges toward it and sucks hungrily. While he does that, I ask Chris to get the applesauce, and then everything slows down. Within a few minutes, Jake is much quieter. It's not perfect. He's fussy. There's applesauce on my shirt and the seat in front of me. But it's nothing a wet wipe can't handle. When I look around, I see that all of the passengers are absorbed by their cell phones, tapping away. Not one person is looking at us with our screaming kid.

———

A few hours later, we're sitting in lawn chairs on the beach. We're the only ones, because the weather is cloudy and cold, and it looks like it might rain any second.

"Well, this is ironic," I say.

Chris pulls his fleece tighter over his neck. "Yep. You got your deserted beach."

I ignore the jab, running my fingers over my cheeks, which feel soft and supple. "At least this moisture feels good."

He smiles. "True." Colorado is painfully arid in the winter.

A man delivers cocktails to the table that separates us. My drink has an umbrella in it. I take a long sip of the sweet clear liquid, noting the strong presence of vodka. *Bring it on.* I'm exhausted after this day, like I would be if I'd hiked a long trail carrying a forty-pound pack, some combination of physical weariness from changing environments, and mental strain from keeping track of my belongings and watching for danger in a foreign landscape. The drink is refreshing. I silently give the mom from the airport a "cheers." She's probably got her Mai Tai right now, winding down just like me.

As I slurp my drink, downing it too fast and looking for the server to order another, it occurs to me that this trip is not an *un-adventure* at all. The adventure is simply not what I expected. It had nothing to do with the destination. Rather, it was about the airplane ride—the seemingly no-brainer task of boarding a plane and entering the unknowns of air travel with a baby, surviving from point A to point B—something that barely even registered as part of the travel experience before kids, when I jetted off to Germany or Costa Rica. It's yet another thing I didn't anticipate about motherhood–how flying would loom as a hurdle, requiring me to conjure up bravery. How something that was a means to an end pre-baby could transform into an opportunity for self-exploration.

As I sit on the beach, I feel a sensation of increased confidence rising up in my core. Maybe it's the alcohol bolstering me, but it strikes me as something that will linger once my buzz wears off. It makes me think of our adventure list, which is still sitting under a pile of other papers and manuals at home. It's time to dig out that list. And even though Florida is certainly nowhere on there, I decide to add a bullet that says "Sanibel," because this has been, in fact, an important motherhood stepping stone, a developmental stage that parallels Jake's milestones. *Jake smiles. Jake sprouts teeth. Carrie travels by airplane with her baby.* The idea of what this symbolizes and what lies ahead, excites me.

Jake fusses and I set him down in the sand. I roll off my chair and lie next to him, sifting the fine grains through my fingers and toes. Jake reaches for a shell and picks it up. He stares at it, mesmerized, his eyes practically crossed with focus and fascination. In response, I pick up a snail and stare at it cross-eyed, mirroring Jake. The fine lines, like the ones on my palm, run together into a blur.

"What are you doing?" Chris asks.

I giggle. "Seeing what Jake sees."

Chris wrinkles his nose. "You're weird." But then he can't resist. He joins us in the sand and picks up a pinkish shell and crosses his eyes.

We begin to giggle uncontrollably, crossing our eyes and staring at our shells, Jake, and each other, reveling in our dizziness. Being silly. I can't remember the last time I acted like a kid. Certainly I've never acted like a nine-month-old. It's pretty fun.

Jake crawls around, picking up shells, smelling and licking them, and then he stops in his "modeling pose," an adorable position he's recently adopted where he leans on one elbow, both legs extended to his side, smiling up, like he's posing for an advertisement. This makes us laugh even harder.

I collapse on my back, smiling, staring up at the sky. Chris rolls next to me and kisses my neck. It feels delicious. I throw my leg over his body. It's one of the only spontaneous intimate moments we've shared since Jake was born, and I sigh, embracing it.

Jake crawls over and worms his way between us. "Mama," he says. I kiss his nose. He puts his hand in mine. I squeeze. He squeezes back.

"I love you," I say, speaking to both of my guys at once.

We lay there, the three of us entangled, silent. In this moment, I feel totally content, both as a wife and a mom. This was one of my goals. And suddenly, maybe because of the vodka and the length of the day, I feel so exhausted I can no longer keep my eyes open. It's a bone-deep exhaustion—nine-months-into-motherhood tired. With that, I surrender into the sand and my family and my fluffy adventure, close my eyes, and let the sea breeze begin its process of rejuvenation.

7

One Moment in Life

One Year into Motherhood

It's not until I'm halfway through my question that I realize I may be offending my new Turkish friend.

"Abdul," I say. "Do the women in this village do all the work?"

We're sitting across from each other in an open-air café near Bozalan, Turkey sipping yellow tea from tiny hourglasses. From our place on the balcony, weathered buildings traipse downhill in notched angles to the shores of the Aegean Sea.

Abdul, who is the *Kaptan* of our boat, looks at me and rubs his white-flecked mustache. I resist the urge to tug on my frizzy hair which is tangled from the salt water that doesn't exist at home.

"Carrie, why do you think this?" Abdul asks.

He's smiling, and I gesture at the dozen men sitting around us in the café. It is the middle of the day, and they're drinking tea and playing a game that looks like Scrabble, except the clinking tiles are etched with numbers instead of letters. In contrast, on our walk up the hill to the café, the only women I glimpsed were behind windows or on porches, chasing pudgy-cheeked toddlers or weaving intricate Turkish rugs.

I state the obvious. "Well, there are only men at this café, and the women I've seen are at home, working."

Abdul frames his face with calloused hands. He nods. "It looks that way, maybe."

I stir my tea, waiting.

"But Carrie, this is one moment in life."

I glance from his eyes to his forehead. His bushy eyebrows make him look wise, like a sage. "Hmm," I say.

Abdul taps his hand on the table like he's playing the piano. His face turns playful.

I cock my head to the side. "I'll have to think more about that."

He stands up. "You think while I go to the restroom."

I smile and sit back in my chair, sipping my tea, staring at the rich, dark wood of our table. Below, one of my flip flops has slipped off, and I leave it there, tucking my bare foot underneath me, and stretching my arms overhead. A woman with long hair and a bold patterned skirt flows across the floor and serves a tray of tea to a quartet of men who have just arrived.

I think back to a couple of months earlier, when I discovered this adventure online. I was clicking around on my computer while Jake napped, snowflakes floating to the ground outside my window. Jake had finally transitioned from a swing to a crib, and that meant he spent longer times in his room. But it was only partly about sleep. He was totally into his crib's jungle gym properties, using the bars to pull himself up and around, holding onto the railing and wiggling his hips in a funny dance, and occasionally sleeping. I was okay with his shenanigans, because

I liked that he was learning to entertain himself independently. A useful life skill.

That day, I'd watched through the crack in the door while Jake sat in his crib quietly, eyes open, leaning against the bars, pressing his hands together and then pulling them away, repeating this over and over. His face lit up, and then I realized why: He'd learned to clap. I wanted to leave—his naptime was an opportunity to get a list of things done like laundry, cleaning, shoveling, a yoga set, or procrastinating from all of the above by searching the internet—but I couldn't stop smiling and staring. I stood peering through his door thinking, *Wow. This is one of the most delightful things I've ever observed in my life.*

In the last months, I'd begun to embrace the amazement of raising a child. With only one part time job—writing—I had more time to linger in the present, and the haze of postpartum depression had finally lifted, my butchered-up pills taking full effect and restoring the uptake of neurotransmitters in my cells to seemingly-normal levels. It was like I'd emerged from a cocoon to a new me. Or maybe it was simply the old me, revised. I wasn't exactly sure. What I knew was that I could finally think clearly again. It made me realize how terribly I'd been doing for all of those months.

Finally leaving Jake to clap on his own, I closed his door, glanced at the pile of laundry the size of Everest, decided to ignore my responsibilities (just for ten minutes, right?) and opened my computer, landing on a women's clothing site, even though I didn't need anything. Romeo jumped onto my lap, snuggling his head into my belly, happy to have any time alone with me. As I clicked around on yoga pants and cute scoop-necked T-shirts, I noticed an ad had popped up on the side of my screen promoting a stroller fitness class. The picture showed a group of model-thin women in spandex doing quadriceps stretches, holding their strollers for balance.

Ugh. It reminded me of the last time I'd been at the mall, looking for a bra. I hated the mall, but it was impossible to buy a bra online. I mean, seriously, had *What to Expect When You're Expecting* said to expect to buy bras in every single size, material, and shape to accommodate an ever-changing bust? My bra collection looked like it was owned by four different women. I'd parked in a spot designated Parents with Babies, in the front row (Walmart could learn from this), put Jake in his secondhand stroller, and entered the mall through one of the lesser-used entrances. Inside the doors, I immediately felt like I'd landed in a foreign country. A dozen women were standing in a circle doing tricep dips on the planters, which had fake plants inside, and the teacher was playing 1970's dance music. Their infants and toddlers were strapped into their strollers, drinking out of sippy cups, munching on goldfish crackers out of spill-proof containers, bobbing their heads or wiggling their feet to the beat, and staring at each other.

I overheard two women talking, slightly breathless, complaining about their partners. One woman's husband didn't help with *anything*. ("I mean, he's changed about three diapers, total.") The other woman's partner—he wasn't her husband, thank God—was about to leave on a week-long ski trip with his buddies. He didn't even ask about her schedule.

Nothing against stroller fitness, but sort of like the concept of exposing my breast in public while nursing, I knew this wasn't my thing. I had no desire to do squats against the back of Jake's stroller, while bitching about Chris to a fellow participant. I liked hiking in the fresh air among real plants.

So I jogged right through the stroller fitness class, dodging a red Peg Pérego and a black double Graco, channeling my racing days from high school track, avoiding eye contact, dashing to the finish line, which was (oddly) the entrance to Victoria's Secret. Yet as I browsed through the bras, pulling a lacy black demi out of the sale bin and actually considering purchasing it, I had to admit something was bothering me. Despite my lack of interest, the women in that stroller fitness class looked fit and content, and who was I to judge what they were discussing? I realized I was jealous. Those women had friends with common interests, and although I had a handful of mom friends—a few writers and a neighbor—it wasn't an organized thing. The women in that class had found their tribe. Where was mine?

Maybe I thought they were floating on the Aegean Sea, because I clicked off the women's clothing site (goodbye stroller fitness ad) and began typing in keywords that made me stop feeling envious and judgmental toward others and instead resonated deeply with my own internal landscape. I typed: Ocean, Eco, Trek, and Travel. This brought me to the headline: "Writing Workshop Sailing Off the Coast of Turkey."

Now this *was* what I was looking for. Captivated, thinking about Chris's recent suggestion that I plan an adventure for myself now that Jake was older, I sped through the description: Seven days sailing the Aegean Sea on a traditional Turkish *gulet* (which is like a pirate ship!), swimming in the sea, doing daily writing exercises, meeting one-on-one with the writing teacher, and visiting ancient ruins. Turkey evoked mystery and sensuality, and I had never been anywhere in the Mediterranean before. It might be the perfect place to reconnect with my inner femininity, just like Cleopatra. I could delve into a creative writing project, maybe start the book that was on my mind. And perhaps I'd discover my tribe, if they existed. The thought of the trip met not one, but *two* of the priorities I'd identified since becoming a mother: writing and adventure. And it was definitely an item on the adventure list. I could already feel the sand squishing between my toes, the strings of my bikini grazing my thighs, and taste flakes of fresh fish on my tongue. I could hear the pages of my journal blowing in the wind below the ship's sail.

Then, as if on cue, Jake woke up from his nap (or clapping fest). His cries yanked me straight off the *gulet*. I tossed Romeo off my lap, shut down my computer, and wandered downstairs to comfort him.

"Hey, darling," I said, lifting him out of his crib. His body was warm and sweet-smelling, and I cradled him in our glider chair, stroking his sparse hair and kissing his pale nose. I thought about Turkey. It was then that the guilt began to blossom. I thought, *But how can I leave Jake?* I calculated the logistics of the trip in my mind. Between flights and layovers and the time difference, I'd have to be gone for at least eleven days. *Practically forever.* I wanted an adventure, but didn't a trip to Turkey seem frivolous compared to my beautiful baby boy?

I was still having trouble leaving Jake for one day. In addition to help from grandparents, Chris and I had found a great in-home daycare, and we'd enrolled him two days a week. It was hard every time I dropped him off. He bawled and reached for me, and I thought, *This is agonizing!* I never anticipated phenomena like separation anxiety, and how it would tug at my heart; emotions so strong they threatened to trump my fierce independence.

Yet I knew daycare was good for him. Sometimes I'd arrive early to pick Jake up, just so I could observe his interactions with his playmates from a distance. He was so cute, passing toys to other kids, chomping on a bagel for a snack, pulling up on the sofa, interacting with toddlers in some secret language, communicating with friends who were both older and younger. But what struck me the most was the incredible skill of his daycare provider, Mary. One day I watched her intervene in a "crisis." One toddler had stolen a toy El Camino from another, sending the car-less kid into crying spasms. Mary walked slowly over to the thief and said something like, "Now Seth, was that a nice thing to do?"

Seth looked at her sheepishly.

"And Bethany," she said, addressing the other kid. "How do you use your words to ask for the toy back?"

My jaw dropped in admiration. Two seconds ago, I'd been ready to pounce, thinking, *Man, that Seth kid sure is a little brat. Bethany should clock him right in his crooked little nose. If she won't do it, I will.*

It was clear evidence that Mary was in the right profession and I ought to take notes.

So I knew Jake was benefitting from his daycare, and who could argue the value of him spending time with his grandparents, or alone with Chris. Deep down, I knew I needed to go to Turkey. My friend's words came to mind from when we were riding horses. *You might just have to leap.* This was a new kind of leap–something that felt, because of the immense guilt, just as big as my decision to have a baby in the first place.

When I told Chris about the trip, he was undaunted.

"How can I support you in return?" I asked. He mentioned something about the half marathon he wanted to train for, and we shook hands jokingly. He started carving out a jogging schedule the next day.

Later, Chris admitted that his unabashed support of the trip was more selfish than I might've guessed. "Honestly, I wanted my courageous wife back," he said. "It was your kind of trip. I wanted you to go and come back with stories." I thought about his words and realized it was his way of rekindling of our wedding vows—to honor each other's dreams. He was reminding me that I was a woman with passion, and he liked that. This was a big piece of what made *us* work, what kept our relationship fresh. My trip to Turkey would actually be good for our marriage.

It was decided: I sent in my deposit. This held my place on the pirate ship. A huge adventure awaited.

———

In the café in Turkey, Abdul returns from the restroom and settles into his chair. He picks up the conversation right where we left off—about women working and men playing—as if he'd continued thinking about it while he was peeing and washing his hands and straightening his mustache in the mirror; as if we'd never stopped.

He gestures toward the buildings of Bozalan, elaborating on men's and women's roles in Turkish culture. "Carrie," he says. "Men and women have different roles in this country." He says that men are mostly responsible for the tasks "outside" of the house, such as growing vegetables, raising cattle, and negotiating rug prices with dealers. Women have authority over things "inside" the house like cooking, weaving rugs and caring for the children. "Which is why you see them there," he explains.

Abdul adds that Turkish culture varies between regions and within families. In this particular village, the women prefer to socialize at each other's houses, while men enjoy gathering at cafés.

As Abdul talks, my mind drifts back to Colorado. Right now Chris is feeding Jake breakfast before dashing to daycare and then to his job. He's doing "inside" and "outside" jobs the whole time I'm gone, and I feel really fortunate.

I consider the similarities in gender roles between Turkish and American culture: American men still work more often outside the house, and women tend to be responsible for cooking and cleaning. When children are born, American men are not required to change their lifestyles. Many do. Chris is my equal partner in parenting. But if a man travels for work or fun, even for long periods of time, or does risky things like snowboard out of bounds or climb K2, it's accepted as "normal things men do." As for women? Unless she's doing something that directly benefits her family, it's harder to legitimize.

When I told people I was going to Turkey, a few friends were enthusiastic, but most seemed baffled. They said things like, *You're leaving Jake for two weeks? Who's going to care for him? Do you realize Turkey borders Iraq? Are you taking a gun?*

For starters, I told them that Bozalan, Turkey is a thousand miles from Iraq. As for childcare, my husband was coordinating the schedule while I was gone. It took a lot of effort. He and I sat down with our calendars before I left and discussed the options. It was like putting together a 500-piece puzzle: a mind-boggling combination of extended family helping out, increased time at the in-home daycare, and Chris taking time off work to bond one-on-one with Jake. Deep down, I hoped my time away might actually be good for Jake, because I've always believed in the concept that "it takes a village to raise children." Wouldn't my time away allow Jake valuable experiences with "the village"?

But inside, I continued to feel paralyzed by guilt. It seemed there was always some scary feeling burgeoning in my belly; it had simply morphed from fear about having a baby to overcoming the need to have it all to its latest form: guilt. And as usual, it got worse when I listened to outside voices. In this case, people who were skeptical about my plans. When I told one acquaintance about my upcoming trip, she looked at me like I'd lost my mind. Another said, "I would never leave my baby for two weeks," as if I were abandoning my child on a street corner. Yet another suggested I'd better leave a long list of instructions for Chris. "I have to leave my husband a two-page list when I leave for an hour," she said. Inside, I rolled my eyes. This seemed like another example of martyrdom. I wanted to ask her, "Are you making that list for him, or for you?" I wondered if these women were seriously questioning my decision, or if they secretly felt jealous, just like I'd been after seeing the stroller fitness class. Did they want to do what I was doing, but were too paralyzed to jump?

It occurs to me that my original question to Abdul had everything to do with irritation and guilt—irritation I felt about having to justify, as a woman, my desire to be adventurous, while leaving my child with my husband. And guilt because leaving Jake really was as hard as I thought it would be. I was on edge for a whole week before I left, telling Jake over and over that I was only leaving for a little while, and that I'd definitely be back. He stared at me, smiling, completely clueless. It bothered me that he was too young to understand. I worried that he really would think I had abandoned him on a street corner.

Then, when Chris and Jake dropped me off at the airport with my svelte red carry-on/backpack combo, I squeezed Jake's little hand in his car seat, waited for him to squeeze back, went inside and practically hyperventilated in the airport bathroom. I thought I had worked through it all, taking in people's reactions and letting them go, allowing myself time at home to wallow in guilt and self-doubt and sadness, but maybe these are the kinds of emotions you shove out to sea, and sometimes they float back with the tide.

———

We exit the café and begin the descent from the village back to the boat. I take in the lush landscape—pine trees mixed with sage and flowering shrubs. The air is richly aromatic and sensuous. My skirt swooshes against my knees, flip flops tapping the ground like gentle drum beats. The fabric of my shirt drapes loosely over my breasts. As the road descends sharply, I brace myself against the steep rocky ruts. Again, I feel the presence of my core muscles—little fires in my belly, a slight burning in my inner thighs. My center is stronger, and I stop, close my eyes, and turn my chin up to the sky, letting the sunshine fill me all the way through. In this moment, I feel fully alive. More like a Mediterranean goddess than an American mother. This is why I came here. This is what I needed. It's a beautiful milestone; something I will add to my adventure list, right under Sanibel.

Abdul appears at my side. He picks a yellow bloom off a flowering bush and offers it to me. "For you, Carrie," he says.

"Thank you, *Kaptan*." I tuck it behind my ear. This simple act—receiving a flower from a gentleman and placing it in my hair—feels divine. I can feel my cheeks glowing pink.

Abdul glances at the flower and smiles. He faces me. "I think it's brave that you're here," he says.

I smile. "Really?"

He nods. "I meet lots of people on my *gulet*," he says. "But I've never met a woman quite like you—as adventurous and vibrant. I mean, you sleep outside every night!"

I laugh. It's true I take my blankets and pillow on deck at dusk, write in my journal by the light of my headlamp, and sleep under the stars. Everyone else on this trip—mostly women—are tucked down below. Even my shipmates who don't have children have mentioned how much they admire my spirit. They've nicknamed me "Girl Scout." One twenty-something woman from California said to me, "If I have kids someday, I want to do just what you're doing." Another, a mother of two grown children, says my forays remind her of her solo travels when her kids were young. As we spend time together bonding, jumping from the ship's deck into the water, sharing our writing and stories, and laughing over wine and fruit plates, I realize these women are my tribe. They're not typically all in one place, like in a stroller fitness class or a mommy group, and they're not even all mothers. It's more of a global community, a collection of people who embrace and understand what it means to be a person who craves adventure. And I suppose that's natural. People with wanderlust gather out in the world.

Even with all this support, I still wonder if Abdul's words are true. *Am I really brave? Is it good to honor my core? Or am I a selfish brat?*

Just as I begin to think, *Yes, Abdul's right, I am brave, and this is good for me, Chris, and Jake,* I notice a group of children sitting on some concrete stairs that lead up to a house. They're toddlers with black hair and brown eyes, wearing clothes in bright hues—red dresses, blue shorts, white shirts. "*Merhaba,*" they shout in greeting. I wave. Without warning, I long for Jake so deeply my heart squeezes tight like a fist. Suddenly, I can't catch my breath, and Jake's face fills my mind. But his features are vague—his blue eyes smeared over his nose, like an abstract painting. My pulse thumps and I pant and wonder, *Have I already forgotten my son? I can't see his face! How come I can't see his face? I need to see his face! What if he's already forgotten me?!* The flower slips from my hair. I catch it before it hits the ground and shove it back behind my ear, but the act pushes me off balance, like I am once again pregnant, my center tipped forward, in my womb. I extend my hands and brace myself for a fall.

Abdul grabs my arm and yanks. "Carrie!" he yelps.

I blow air out of my mouth.

"Are you okay?"

I plant my feet solidly on the ground and nod, looking down.

For a second, time stops.

Abdul points to the kids. "They remind you of your son," he states.

I bite my bottom lip.

He nods. "The same thing happens to me when I sail on long trips." He pulls a photo out of his pocket. It's his family. His wife is beautiful, with cascading dark hair, and his children resemble him closely.

I smile. "They're lovely," I say. "All of them."

"Yes. I really love them." He pauses, his eyes boring into mine. "And I love sailing. I need to be out on my own."

We stare at each other for a few seconds, silent, knowing. The air becomes confused, unexpectedly charged, and I step back, surprised. I'm not physically attracted to Abdul, but in this moment—two souls connecting —I suddenly find myself thinking: What if I'd married a man like him? Someone who'd whisk me (and our child) off to exotic places, dedicated to a life of global explorations? Did I do the right thing by marrying a man who is perfectly content at home?

It's the same question I had when Chris and I decided to get married—that little piece of doubt—resurfacing. I didn't expect it to come up, especially now of all times, but here it is. Abdul and I stand there caught in a sea of electromagnetic particles.

He looks down at the picture. This small movement clears the air, and I sense that we're both thankful. I push those wayward thoughts out of my mind. I stand up straight.

"Carrie, it's good that you're an American woman," Abdul says.

"Yes," I say, quickly. But then I take in the weight of his words, which speak volumes. *I am an American woman.* Which means I can get frustrated with maternity leave policies or cultural norms, or the fact that my desire to travel solo baffles people, but no one is stopping me. Adventure is my choice. Who I marry is my choice. Irritation and guilt are my own emotions. The only thing standing in my way is *me*. This is empowering and scary all at the same time.

As Abdul and I continue walking down the hill, I think about how solo travel is a mixed bag now that Jake is part of my life— moments of much-needed independence laced with the tug of that invisible cord connecting me to my son, like the umbilical cord was never truly cut. The pendulum of emotions occasionally pulls me overboard. But as Abdul says, everything is just "one moment in life."

Abdul puts a hand on my shoulder. It reminds me of something my dad would do—polite and gentle and kind. As we walk side-by-side, I feel deeply connected to him in a way I've rarely felt with anyone. I know without knowing that we will lose touch after this trip, but we will always have this moment, and he will be part of my global community.

Abdul gestures up ahead, to where I can barely see the shores of the sea.

"What's up there?" I ask.

"The *gulet*," he says, smiling.

"Oh, I see it. I think."

He begins to walk faster, and I follow in step.

"Carrie," he says. "It is time to get back on the boat."

I smile at the metaphorical value of his words. "That's right," I say. And I do exactly that; I get back onto the *gulet*, and I continue my adventure, flowing with the tide, in the waves of the unpredictable sea.

8

Lay That Baby Down

Fourteen Months into Motherhood

I stand in my driveway straddling a motorcycle. It's a 2008 Harley Davidson Sportster: 750 cc engine, black and chrome body, impeccably maintained. As the sun warms the back of my black jacket, which is embossed with some badass symbol I don't really understand but makes me look legit, five hundred pounds of metal vibrates between my thighs. It takes all of my concentration to hold the bike upright, and I plant my boots firmly in the gravel, centering the weight.

The engine rumbles loud and louder, and I roll the throttle, warming it up. *Vroom*, it screams. *Vroooom*. The sound is deafening, blocking out the voices of nature around our property–birds, grasshoppers, the rushing river. Chris stands near the garage, holding Jake in his arms. They stare at me, smiling, but Chris's eyes flash concern. Jake's glow pure joy.

Even though Jake is only a toddler, he is all *guy*. I'm eternally struck by the stereotypical presence of his Y-chromosome. Although I've introduced him to a wide range of books and toys to see what engages him, his choices certainly make a case for the "nature" part of the "nature versus nurture" conversation. No matter how many dolls and stuffed animals surround him at daycare, in his crib, or in the library playroom, he'll grab for a toy car. Or a train. Or the collection of diggers.

Today, Jake looks at me like I'm the most amazing woman he's ever seen, his toes wiggling with joy. And because he doesn't yet know about cultural gender roles, he doesn't realize that although women do ride motorcycles, it would be more common for Chris to be out here in the driveway. I love that. I roll the throttle again, smiling over at him, sticking out my tongue in a funny face that makes him giggle. And then I re-focus. I think about what's ahead. It's not just the engine that's warming up—it's me, my mind. I'm about to take my motorcycle out on the longest ride of my life.

I found this bike on Craigslist a month ago. I'd been searching through ads, finding most motorcycles too expensive or mechanical nightmares, but this one looked good for a casual rider like me; only one owner (a woman), garage-kept, low miles, and an even lower price to get rid of it fast. I called Chris and begged him to take a long lunch and drive the thirty miles with me to look at it.

Chris balked on the phone. "I don't even know what to say. I didn't know you *liked* motorcycles."

"Come on. It'll be good for me. To do something new." Of course, a stroller fitness class would've also been new. Or joining a mommy group.

He was silent.

"Just think of the romance. We can ride to the movie theater.

Or along Highway 1 in California. You can learn to ride, too. Or you can ride on the back!"

He snickered. "Never."

"We can ride around Bali!"

"What are you talking about? Bali?"

"Do you know that in Bali they haul their entire families around on motorcycles?"

Silence.

"Remember, you like that I'm adventurous?" I tried.

"Okay, I'll go with you to look at the bike," he said. "But you know how I feel."

Which is true. As clearly as I know Chris loves football, running, and skiing, I understand he *does not* like motorcycles. The road in front of our house is often cluttered with rumbling bikes of all shapes and sizes on the weekends, a common route for people touring the foothills. He hates all the noise. Also, I've heard him refer to motorcycles more than once as "death machines."

When we arrived at the owner's house on the high plains, the bike was, in fact, beautiful. I couldn't help asking why she was selling it. She patted her bulging belly and said, "I don't have time to ride anymore. I'm due in six weeks. I need to buy a stroller and car seat."

I hadn't even noticed she was pregnant, because I was too caught up in the shining beauty of the bike, already imagining myself as the new owner. I'd need to get some saddlebags to store a few things while I rode. And what about boots? And gloves?

Chris looked at me sideways, in the way that suggested he was beginning The List in his mind. "Well, she's a mom, too," he said, pointing at me. "Our son is just over a year. And we're thinking about a second."

The woman recoiled. "Really?"

I nodded.

"There's no way you're going to have time," she said. "I mean, I want to sell you my bike, but do you feel comfortable riding as a mom?"

I ignored her, thinking, *plenty of responsible mothers ride motorcycles*. I didn't really know any, but I knew they were out there. There had to be a Motorcycle Mama group. Right?

I also ignored the words of the instructor who taught my two-day "How to ride a motorcycle class" at the local community college. She encouraged all of us, even the tough tattooed nineteen-year-olds who'd been riding without a license for years, to start off with a small bike. "Do not even think about buying a Harley right away," she said, reading all of our minds. "They're really heavy and you're gonna dump it. Or at least lay it down."

I didn't know what "dump" or "lay it down" meant, except that it was clearly a bad idea. But I smirked at her with the other students and pretended only some dumbass would do that. As she talked, I studied the diagram in the workbook. While she lectured about wearing reflective clothing and not riding in the rain, I studied the basics, the stuff everyone else took for granted. I knew absolutely nothing. I didn't know how to shift gears with my foot, or what the choke was for, or even where to put in gas.

The learning curve for me was steep, and I had two days to figure it all out. Because I'm good at memorization, from my German and Spanish studies, and from genetic mapping, I got a perfect score on the paper/pencil version of the test. But my performance in the parking lot during the practical exam, riding a small bike around orange cones, over bumps, and through pretend stop signs, reminded me of the time Chris and I rented a car to drive the mountain roads of Costa Rica, and I drove about 5 mph, gripping the steering wheel through the obstacle course of potholes, steep ledges, and hairpin curves.

On the motorcycle course, it's not that I crashed or did anything outright embarrassing, but unlike everyone else in the class who was younger or familiar with motorcycles or had a husband who rode, I was pretty tentative and ultra-focused and trembling, and I could tell the instructor was worried about me. She kept furrowing her eyebrows. And she was right to worry: I had no experience to draw from. No one in my family rode. Chris didn't ride. Motorcycle handling skills were not coded into my DNA, and had never been part of my environment.

Which is exactly why I'm doing it, I tell myself, as I roll the throttle of the Harley in my driveway one more time. It's out of my comfort zone; a new country. A way to build my skill base. I have the famous poster of Georgia O'Keeffe hanging in my writing shed, the one where she's riding on the back of a guy's motorcycle in the desert. The caption says, "Women who rode away."

I toss a gloved hand in the air toward Chris and Jake, afraid to take one hand off the handlebars for more than ten seconds. With that, I pull in the clutch, shift to first gear, and roll up the driveway, holding tight through the gravel, which is not a good surface for street bikes. From this direction, our driveway curves slightly uphill and spills out onto a sometimes busy road. It takes precise handling to crest the hill—gravel to asphalt—and then stop on flat ground. I've practiced this lots of times, but I still have to focus, and today I stop in a less-than-perfect position, blocking the bike lane and slightly sideways. I don't look back at Chris, because I know that he's frowning. Instead, I glance left and right for traffic, and because the coast is completely clear in both directions, I pull into the southbound lane, check my mirrors, and shift to second gear–two clicks up with my toe. The bike picks up speed, and then more speed, and then I'm cruising 30 mph, the speed limit. I'm riding away. I take a deep breath, loosening my shoulders, relaxing my grip on the handlebars. "Yeehaw," I yell. And then I start singing one of my favorite songs, the classic by Neil Young, "Somewhere on a desert highway, she rides a Harley Davidson…"

The wind feels good on my face, blowing my hair behind me, out from under my helmet. I think I might look a little bit like a woman in a Harley ad, or at least the cool chicks at the Sturgis Motorcycle Rally. My jacket billows out behind me a bit, and I reach one hand around to smooth it down. Since returning from my trip to Turkey a couple of months ago, I've been feeling so good; alive and vibrant and ready for new things. The adventure totally reenergized me. Chris was exactly right: I came back with bright eyes and fun stories. Even better, Jake didn't seem fazed by my absence. He looked a little confused when he saw me at the airport—I'll never forget his chubby legs toddling toward me near the baggage claim, arms outstretched, eyes squinting in a "Is that really my mama?" kind of way. We shared a very long hug. But Chris said overall they did fine, and within two days we were back to our pre-Turkey routine, Chris embracing the extra breaks I offered for him to sleep in or prepare for the upcoming fantasy football draft.

On this open country road, I travel a series of fences: white picket, barbed wire, stained wood, which enclose donkeys, horses, humans, and miles of open space. I keep my eyes on the road—staying just right of the yellow center line—and try to let my mind go. I try to think about romance and freedom and escape, and how good it feels to be doing this. I'm really doing this! But my mind won't let go. Maybe it's the fences, I don't know, but I go somewhere I don't want to drive: to the conversations Chris and I have been having about a second child. He began bringing it up in earnest immediately post-Turkey, and deep down, I know this is the real reason I bought the bike. I'm having a Baby Crisis, which is probably not so different from the midlife crises that are common among middle-aged men. In my case, Chris is more ready for a baby than I am, again, like he's experiencing the ticking maternal clock that's supposed to be in my chest. The points he brings up are always the same–some version of The List, and it's hard to refute them:

1. It would be nice for Jake to have a sibling. *Yes.*
2. Because if Jake had a sibling, we could watch them interact. *That would be cool.*
3. Wouldn't it be fun to maybe have a girl? *Maybe.*
4. Or another boy. A brother for Jake. *Maybe.*
5. The longer we wait to have a second child, the harder it will be to go back.

This last point, Number 5, is the real kicker. It's the one that grates at me because the reality is that most of me already feels like I'm at a point of no return. As in, *I feel good, finally,* and I have no desire to go back to nurturing a newbie in the needy dependent infant stage. I have no desire to be pregnant again. I don't really want to dive back into muumuus and burp cloths and feeding logs and concerns about Down Syndrome and cystic fibrosis, especially since it seems like I just finally stopped worrying about them with Jake. And now I'm even older—thirty-five, advanced maternal age. After one of my conversations with Chris, I couldn't help but pull out my genetic counseling binder again to look up my risks. If I got pregnant today, I'd be thirty-six when Baby #2 was born, and my chances of having a baby with a chromosomal disorder would be 1/200. Still relatively low, unless you're the *one*.

Most importantly, Jake has actually started doing certain things himself—eating, drinking, walking—suggesting that increased independence might exist in our future, possibly in the not-too-distant months ahead.

At a stop sign, I decide to head right. This will take me deeper into the foothills, further away, around Horsetooth Reservoir, where I can ride for dozens of miles. It's a motorcycle haven—the dams around the reservoir and into the two-store town of Masonville—because it's beautiful terrain: hilly and curvy and scenic. It's also probably for more experienced riders. But I've been practicing, even going out a couple of times with friends who gave me some good tips and complimented my quick learning. This route will challenge me; I want to master the art of riding tight curves and steep hills. Plus, I am living an adventurous life! For some reason, I say this out loud, even though it's cheesy: "I am an adventurer!"

But what if we have another baby? Will we be able to

continue exploring—hiking and camping? How are we going to haul everything? Backpacking with one child is one thing, but what about two? Are we going to have to buy one of those giant family-sized tents that weighs as much as this motorcycle? My mind flashes forward to images of gear piles as tall as mountains.

When I tossed out the idea of having a second child to random people, in a purely hypothetical way, but was totally real, they said stuff like, *One kid is a part-time job, two is full time.* Or, *one plus one equals three.* The phrases really annoyed me—the cutesy tone and powerlessness. And then a fellow world traveler said, "Everyone I know pretty much stops traveling with two. It gets really hard, Carrie. It gets expensive. Think of buying four plane tickets versus two."

In fact, I hadn't thought about the expense. How could we go to Bali? Four plane tickets would cost close to $8,000, more than the grand total of our savings account. The motorcycle felt like a much cheaper adventure. Plus, if I didn't like it, it would still be a good investment. Harleys are known to retain their value over time.

I ride up a long winding hill, taking in the views of the reservoir—people boating and waterskiing and a couple of jet skis. I drive and drive, feeling increasingly confident as I navigate long curves with ease, leaning into them while counter steering, as I was taught in my class.

Things are going well, but I can feel myself tiring, and I know from my manual that this is when most accidents happen, so I stop at an overlook to rest and check out the view. In the parking lot, I hit the "Off" switch on my bike, push down the kickstand, and swing my leg over the bike, feeling a little bit bow-legged; the same way I feel after riding horses. I stride over to the vista, my boots shuffling through sand, unzip my jacket, whip off my helmet and shake out my hair. The sun is hot and high, illuminating the water, which sparkles like a watercolor painting.

A guy walks by in the other direction. "Nice day for a ride," he says, smiling.

I nod. "Yeah."

He stops near a pickup truck. "That your Hog?" he asks, gesturing at my bike.

I glance over. "Yeah."

"Pretty nice."

"Thanks."

"And you're out here alone?"

I shrug. "Uh huh."

He shakes his head and laughs. "Tough chick."

This makes me smile and puff out my chest. But as he pulls away in his pickup and I glance back out at the water, I swallow a lump in my throat. The truth is, I don't feel like a tough chick at all. Really, I'm a scared woman. I'm a mother who's grappling for her identity in an impossible match. A woman who's avoiding what's next, while the inevitable waits, laughing. In moments like this, I genuinely wish I were more like Chris, content as a homebody, or at least like other mothers who sell their motorcycles instead of buying them as they expand their families.

Frustrated, I exit the turn-out and head home. At a key intersection, I have the choice to go two different ways. One will take me the long winding way back to my house. The other heads down a very steep hill that exists in two parts. It culminates in a flat road on the south side of the football stadium at Colorado State University.

I opt for the epic descent, because I want to test my skills. At first, all goes well. Instead of riding my brakes—wearing them out—I downshift into third, and then second, gear. I descend very slowly, and although I'm aware that there are cars behind me, probably cursing at my slow speed, I don't let it bother me. I want to keep myself safe. I know my limits, and that I'm pushing them just by choosing this route.

At the end of the first part of the hill, there's a stop sign, which is a T-intersection. From my experience on my road bike, I know it's a tricky stop, because the pavement isn't flat; it's at a weird angle, the road surface uneven. I hope to slow down and then cruise right through, keeping my momentum going. It looks like I'm in the clear, but then a car creeps up from the left and it's too close to avoid stopping. *Oh well*, I think, and I press in the hand brakes and push down on the rear brakes. I stop slowly, beautifully, and I am busy congratulating myself on my deft use of braking, when I realize just how uneven the surface is under my feet. As I stand there, the bike's engine rumbling, watching the car go by, my bike leans heavily to the right. I brace and *brace* against the full weight of the bike, trying to hold all quarter of a ton with one leg. My core muscles fire, and fire harder, burning in my abdomen, and my thigh trembles. "Ugh!" I shout, like I am trying to win an arm wrestling match. Slowly, slowly, my leg and core muscles cry "uncle" in surrender. In slow motion, the bike drops to the right. Just in time, I jump off and pounce into the grass so it doesn't crush my leg. The bike lays there. *Laid down. Dumped.*

Standing there, shocked at my situation, I can feel eyes on me, burning through my helmet. I look up. Two trucks are pulled over at the stop sign. A guy jumps out and runs to my side. He's wearing a cowboy hat and boots and has a deep scar on his cheek. He looks to be about twenty. "Are you okay?" he asks.

I nod, trying to look okay. I shift my feet in the ditch, rubbing my hands over my arms and jeans, feeling like I must be injured somewhere, waiting to feel a spot that's tender or broken or bleeding, but of course I am completely unscathed. I didn't crash, after all. It's just my ego that's hurt. I'm embarrassed, but it's much worse than that. *Death machine*, I think. *What if? What if? What if? What if I died and couldn't go home to Jake? What if I died and couldn't have another baby?* My motorcycle continues rumbling like a huge injured exotic creature, an elephant or rhino, like it refuses to accept that it's down. The guy flips the "Off" switch. The beast now looks dead.

He looks over at me. "You sure you're okay?" He scans my body, but in a way that's polite, like my doctor.

"Yeah," I say. "I'm fine."

He shakes his head. "This is the worst intersection. I've almost dumped here so many times. I avoid it at all costs when I'm on my Ninja."

This makes me feel ever so slightly better, but I'm still mad. Mad that I failed. Mad that I chose to ride terrain, alone, that was beyond my ability, putting myself at risk. Mad that this stupid machine beat me, when I was the one who needed to conquer my fears.

"Well," he says. "Let's get you up."

He stands slightly below the bike and heaves it up, biceps rippling. He grunts loudly and I just stand there in awe, like he is the Incredible Hulk, wishing I could help in some way, remembering that this concept did come up in my class—how to lift a bike off its side—but I don't remember at all what we were taught. When the guy has the bike upright, he straddles it, puts it in neutral, and walks it over to flat ground, which is just past the stop sign.

I scurry over. "Thank you so much!" I say. It is only now that I notice my helmet is askew, tipped forward, and I'm still wearing my goggles. I must look hilarious. Nothing like a Harley ad. Not even close to the hot chicks at Sturgis.

I pull down my goggles and adjust my helmet while the guy scans my bike. "Looks pretty okay," he says. He points at the slightly dented rear view mirror, and a couple of scratches on the side. "Not bad, considering you laid this baby down."

Laid this baby down. I smile at his choice of phrases, thinking that at his young age, he probably has no idea what this means to a mother like me. What I think of is Jake in his footie pajamas, running around the house because he runs everywhere, just before bedtime. I think about reading him books about horses and construction sites in our glider chair, singing lullabies, and then laying him gently in his crib. It's one of my favorite rituals of motherhood; that dusky time of night when we are quiet together, cozy and warm, me and my *boy*, squeezing his hand, and him squeezing back.

In this moment, I want nothing more than to lay my real baby down. To kiss his wiggly feet. And maybe another baby wouldn't be so bad. Maybe I can start to entertain the idea. It might be fun to hold two kids in my chair, watch them kiss each other goodnight. (And maybe even tote them around together on a motorcycle in Bali someday.) Because even though this happened, I'm not angry I bought the bike. As usual, it was my off-the-beaten-path way of thinking through a quandary in my life. This experience will get recorded on the adventure list. *Carrie lays her motorcycle down and thinks about getting laid. Ha.*

"Thank you for your help," I say. And I mean this in so many ways. *Thank you for helping me lift up my bike. Thank you for making sure I'm okay. Thank you for helping me figure out my life.*

"No prob," he says, walking away.

I hit "Start" on my bike, and it fires up, no problem. I wave at the guy and pull back onto the road. In my rearview mirror, I see him salute me.

9

Please Not Nudism Forbidden

Eighteen Months into Motherhood

It's 6:45 a.m. when I first see the naked people. I'm pajama-clad on a ledge outside my cabana in Tulum, Mexico, watching the tangerine sun rise over the Caribbean Sea. On the beach, a fleshy figure catches my eye and I crane my neck to get a better look. A man with gray curls, fully naked, strides through the sand, and then suddenly stops to face the sea. His shoulders and back are the color of baked clay. He lifts his arms over his head in one swift motion and begins to bend and twist in a sequence that might be tai chi. I watch, captivated by his total lack of self consciousness as his skin sags and dangles with the flow of his movements. When he drops down into the splits, I look away.

A nude couple strolls into view. They're short with round bellies and thin legs. Pink goggles hang from the woman's neck. They wade into the sea holding hands, and with one loud yelp they bound through the surf and dive into the waves.

I blink. The scene is a shot of espresso in the lazy light of the morning, and I turn and peek through the full-length screened windows of our cabana. Chris is still sleeping, sprawled out in the white sheets of the bed, draped in mosquito netting. I want to run in and jump on him and squeal, "There are naked people out there!"

But I refrain. We arrived last night, and this is one of the few times we've been away from Jake since he was born. It's our first multi-day trip. Pre-baby, we'd planned to be the kind of parents who left our kid with grandparents on a whim, taking off for weekend trips into the forest, hitting the road to artisan fairs in New Mexico, and jetting off to exotic locations, but that has not been the reality. We've done a few day trips, and an overnight for our wedding anniversary. End of story. Even after all this time, I still feel guilty about leaving Jake, and Chris has a hard time, too. He leaves for his office every morning and only spends a few hours with Jake each day. Their time together is precious.

But we tore ourselves away, knowing this was much-needed. We're hoping for sleep and romance, in no particular order. And maybe to try to conceive a second child? My exclamation about nudity (and tackling Chris awake) would offer nothing useful. Plus, the lodge's web site does state that the beach is "clothing optional," an amenity that's listed quietly next to "sea view" and "jungle setting." I was caught up in the excitement of traveling as a couple far away from our home and visiting an eco-lodge and the Caribbean for the first time—things from our adventure list—and was so busy scrolling through the cabana descriptions and typing in our dates and clicking Reserve Now, and then mentally packing my bikini, that I hadn't really thought about the nude beach.

It's not that I don't like being naked. When we take

backpacking trips, we choose secluded camp spots so we can shed our clothes and soak in the sunshine. It makes me feel free and closer to nature, and I love a fresh breeze blowing across my bare skin. We've even done this a couple of times since Jake was born, baby in tow. We have a favorite spot in the Rawah Wilderness, only a couple hours from our home, which we discovered by chance one day; an isolated paradise next to the river with gurgling water, a sheltered niche for a tent, and an open meadow full of wildflowers.

But public nudity is different. Last winter we visited a hot springs in Northern Colorado that was clothing optional at night, and as we soaked in the natural rock pool among dozens of beer-guzzling nude guests, I wanted more than anything to embrace the healing water. Instead I felt like I was on a college spring break trip, painfully conscious of my body, worrying that people were judging my flabby belly and dimpled butt. *Is that guy staring at me?* I'd catch myself thinking. Or, *How much more can I suck in my stomach?*

When I was in Germany, I visited a few nude saunas, which are common, and I especially enjoyed the spa-like setting of a sauna only a short train ride from my flat in Frankfurt. The property was decorated in a Japanese theme, with lanterns and flags along a nature trail, a big indoor/outdoor pool, hot tubs, optional dry brushing treatments, a solarium, and… several nude saunas of varying temperatures, some with aromatherapy. Although a male friend assured me that "there is nothing sexual about it," I couldn't fully grasp that. American culture equates nudity with sex, and I found it hard to let that go, even in order to fully embrace the customs of a new place. My first time in the nude saunas, I stood for many minutes outside the swinging doors, the border between clothed and naked, trying to get up the courage to walk inside. Finally, I did it, but I kept my towel around me and tried really hard not to make eye contact with anyone else.

Here in Mexico, savoring much-needed alone time with Chris, I've been catapulted into another scene of public nudity, in a very different and beautiful place. I wonder if I can bid my insecurities *adios* and join the carefree nudists.

I start by walking around the property in my pajamas, braless, arms crossed over my chest. As I take in my surroundings, I notice that everything seems to exude raw sensuality. The cabanas are palm-thatched, blending into the deep hues of the jungle foliage. Coconut trees, tall and lithe, dance to a sultry rhythm. Fine sand slips like silk through my toes. The spa, which offers traditional Mayan body treatments and an indigenous sweat lodge ritual called *Temazcal*, is open-air, decorated with dark wood furniture. I covertly look around to see if anyone is staring at me (braless!) but no one, employee or guest, appears to even notice my presence. I drop my hands to my sides. We all sort of blend into the jungle—chameleons—immersed in our own experience.

Near the spa, a white mattress hangs from wooden posts. I sit down on the edge, staring up at the sapphire sky. This place is stripped down, emanating pure rustic romance, and I think about how good it feels to stay in a lodge that mirrors my values: simple accommodations that blend into the environment and candlelit cabanas to protect the sea turtles that lay eggs on the beach. This layer of authenticity helps me melt further into my surroundings. No qualms. At one with my desire to travel with a high level of social consciousness and respect for the environment. I lean back on my elbows, arching my back in one long breath, stretching my toes out in front of me, like a soft, sexy Mayan princess.

I walk down the stairs to the beach and wander along the shoreline. Already the sun is hot on my back. I wonder what time it is—eight? Nine? It doesn't matter, I know, and I try to let go of the schedule that feels cemented into my head: wake up, change Jake's diaper, feed Jake, put Jake down for a nap, and then either work on my computer, shower, work out, do laundry, or all of the above, unless I'm in procrastination-mode while he's sleeping. The days vary a bit, especially on the days when Jake goes to daycare, and I work rigorously on writing projects, but mostly it's the same drill. It feels weird to have zero responsibilities.

I'm not complaining. The beach is all glimmering sand, scattered with eager guests, and I hear people talking in French and German. There are Americans, too, and a few locals. Some couples are clothed, wearing bikinis and board shorts. Others are naked. Many women are topless. A nude family of four sits in a circle, building a sandcastle. Automatically, I cringe. I feel guilty, but secretly, I'd hoped not to see any children at this resort, and I cross my fingers there aren't more. Even though I'm a mom, I support adults-only places, and I crave them, especially when I'm away from my own child.

At the edge of the beach, I see Chris reclined in a chair in khaki shorts, staring at the sea. "Morning," he says.

I kiss him on the cheek. "When did you wake up?"

"A few minutes ago." He yawns and looks up at me. "I figured you'd find me."

I smile shyly. "You look good." I touch his arm, which is

lean and muscled. And then I take in his flat stomach and strong thighs. He's never been out of shape, but right now he's training for a difficult half marathon through the foothills near our home, and he's in extra good condition. I stand there, staring at him. And then it strikes me: *When was the last time I really, truly looked at my husband? Before Jake was born?*

When it comes to my relationship with Chris, I've noticed a tendency to put on the mask that's followed me through life, smiling and telling people our love life hasn't lost a beat since Jake was born; it's as vibrant as when we first met. But that's not true.

Which makes me think about our last romantic evening. We'd been trying to go out once a week, exchanging childcare with friends, in an effort to reconnect as a couple and spark passion and zest in our relationship. I was reading a book about happy relationships instead of happy babies and the author suggested keeping things simple rather than putting pressure on perfection, so we'd chosen dinner and a movie at our favorite independent theater, something we'd loved doing since our dating days in Minneapolis. We liked to play a game we called Film Roulette, which involved choosing a movie without knowing anything about it—not reading the synopsis or the reviews, but liking the title—and just walking in. But on that night, the movie happened to be about a violent psychotic killer who walked around blowing people to pieces. I was horrified and spent most of the two hours hiding under Chris's jacket and wishing to go home to kiss Jake on the cheek.

Afterwards, in bed with Chris, despite my best efforts to surrender, it was the same old thing. I found myself feeling distracted, worried that Jake would wake up and need me, or that

I should be doing something to prepare for the next thing, or the next thing, or making up for something I forgot to do the day before.

But today on the beach there is nothing to worry about. It is all sand and romance and freedom. And us. It sort of feels like a college fling, or a honeymoon. Chris wraps his arms around my hips, pulling me between his legs. "You look well-rested," he says.

I nod. "I slept better than I have in years."

Chris's eyes move from my hair, to my eyes, to my mouth. "You're so beautiful," he says.

I blush. "Aw."

He rests his hands in the curve of my lower back, under my pajama top, and I just stand there, biting my bottom lip, staring at him. "What do you think of this place?" I ask.

His eyes shoot tiny sparks.

I giggle and perch on his lap, placing my hands on his shoulders. He kisses my wrist and runs his tongue up my inner arm. My body tingles in response. "Yum," I say. I snuggle into his chest and let myself lie there, belly relaxed against his, smelling his skin, feeling his fingers dance across my back, relaxing deeper and deeper into this man who I know, yet don't fully remember. Who is the father of my child, yes, but also *my* lover.

After what might be minutes or an hour, Chris breathes deeply, and his exhale pushes my body up to sitting. "Should we swim?" he asks.

"Sure," I say. Unexpectedly, tears fill the corners of my eyes.

Chris straightens and touches my cheeks. "What's wrong?"

"I don't know." I look down, embarrassed.

"What is it?"

I shrug and shake my head. I search his eyes. "I think I've just missed you," I whisper.

We sit in silence for a few moments.

Chris pulls my chin toward him and embraces me in a long, tight hug. He sighs. "Me too."

⸻

We wander back to our cabana to get towels and swimsuits, holding hands, silent, walking slower than I've moved in almost two years. I think of our honeymoon in Costa Rica, which was sensual and sans agenda, just like this. We hauled our backpacks to remote waterfalls and rode horses and drove into the deep jungle and lay in bed for entire days. It feels so long ago. I watch our feet strolling side-by-side in the sand, my bright red toenails next to his pale feet, and I take in the deformed nail on the big toe of his left foot, a consequence of running many miles, over many years. I hadn't noticed it was still broken, trying to heal. I notice Chris doing the same thing with me—stroking my fingers with his—remembering how they feel. He looks down.

"Your hands are so tiny," he says. I smile. He looks up. "Just like your ears." We both laugh. It's true that I have oddly small ears, pixie-like. We used to joke about it a lot.

As I revel in this attention we're giving each other—no distractions or interruptions—I think about how this part of my identity, as Chris's wife and lover, is as essential as anything to making me feel whole. I am an individual, a mother, a wife, and all three need their own special time and attention. When one gets ignored, I feel incomplete. Sometimes I don't even realize what's missing until it stares me in the face. And contrary to the advice from the author of the book about happy relationships, maybe in our case we needed more than a simple night out to reconnect—we needed to travel many miles out of our familiar routine to find each other again.

In the cabana, I sit down on the ground, rifling through my suitcase. "It's weird," I say. "I don't even really miss Jake."

Chris laughs. "I kind of do, but I see him less than you do. But I'm very glad we're here."

"I didn't realize how much we needed it."

Chris puffs up his cheeks and blows out. "I know." He leans into his suitcase, produces his swim trunks and begins to change.

I toss my bikini around in my hands. "Should I wear this?" I ask.

Chris pauses, amused. "Absolutely not."

I laugh. "Really?"

"Really."

"Oh, I don't know." I slide on my bottom, tightening the strings. And then I fasten the top, too. "Maybe I'll ditch it tomorrow."

Chris looks jokingly disappointed.

Back down on the beach, we find a quiet spot near some rock outcroppings for our belongings. I look around. The man who was practicing tai chi is now stacking rocks into intricate towers, wearing only a baseball cap. A tattooed guy in red board shorts sips coffee from a mug. Next to him, a woman sunbathes topless in a chaise lounge, her arms draped over her head. There are two dozen others on the beach. No kids anywhere. Everyone is coupled off, sitting silently, reading or chatting quietly. Unlike the hot springs we visited in Colorado, here there is a general feeling of peace and privacy. The sensuality seeps into my bones.

Chris grabs my hand and pulls me toward the water. "Let's go!"

Digging my toes into the sand, I pull back. "Wait." With a mischievous smile, I loosen the strings of my bikini top.

Chris stops, jaw dropped.

"Are you ready?" In a sweeping, theatrical motion, I toss my bikini to the ground.

Chris beams. "Sweet." He looks at me deeply, grabs my hand, and pulls me toward the water.

As we float in the sea, I embrace the feeling of the waves lapping my shoulders, no strings tugging at my neck, and the deep water offers the seclusion of a campsite, which evokes familiar feelings of freedom. Chris treads water next to me, and he uses the word "paradise" several times to describe our surroundings. I cringe at the cliché, but I have to agree.

After our swim, we dry off in the sun, lying directly on the sand, our bodies making sandy snow angels. And then we spend the rest of the afternoon in our cabana, in bed. Chris only leaves once, to grab us some tacos and beers from the bar.

Later, as I walk on the beach in a sundress before dinner while Chris goes for a jog, I see a wooden sign staked into the sand at the edge of the property. The words "Please Not Nudism Forbidden" are carved into the loose grain. I smile. The person who thrust the sign into the ground probably intended to make a clear point—nudism is evil—but they negated their own rule. Tracing the letters with the tips of my fingers, I consider smearing the "Not" with wet sand to correct it. My inner proofreader can't help it. But as I step back and read it again, I decide to leave it alone. I prefer the sign at face value.

10

What I Wanted

Three Years into Motherhood

The trembling begins at 10 p.m. I'm sitting on a balance ball, rocking side to side, hands interlaced over my belly. Candles light each corner of the room and soft music wafts from the CD player. Although our bedroom is large, containing enough room for a bed and an overstuffed chair, my body appears to dominate the entire space; a palace surrounded by a miniature moat.

A wave pulses through me and I yelp. "Chris," I say. "Get the midwife."

His eyes register alarm. "What? Are you pushing? Is it time?"

"No," I snap. "I don't know. Just get her!"

He rushes down the stairs. From the rhythm of the thumping, it sounds like he's taking them two at a time.

For weeks, Chris has been terrified that I'm going to give birth when he's the only one around. I really can't blame him. In our birthing class, we watched dramatic bloody videos that left us both pale, and we learned mind-blowing foreign words like dilate, transition, and ring of fire. (Johnny Cash's song would never be the same.) Even though this is not my first birth, it *is* my first attempt at a vaginal birth, which has almost nothing in common with a C-section, except the end result. On top of this, I decided I needed to do it at home. Chris has pages of copious notes, a book about being the "birth partner," and he's been timing my contractions on and off for a few days, and diligently since my water broke at dawn.

Out of the corner of my eye, a waif-like presence appears. *Anna. The midwife.* She moves noiselessly, places a bag on the floor at the edge of the room, and stands behind me, resting her hands on my shoulders. "I'm here," she whispers. "You're doing just fine."

"I'm tired," I moan. "I can't stop shaking."

Silence.

"I'm tired," I say louder, in case she didn't hear me.

"Close your eyes," she says, breathing slowly, audibly. "Relax. Do you want to try lying on the bed?"

I look over at the bed, which appears to be about a mile away. "No," I say. I lean forward, head in my hands. A million questions run through my mind that I wish Anna would address. *How am I doing, really? How far am I dilated? What stage of labor am I in? What time, exactly, will my baby be born?* I want her to lead me to the bed, throw open my legs, and use her medical kit to measure and quantify, giving me stats. Dilation: 8. Stage: Transition. Birth time: 11:01 p.m. These are optimistic numbers, I know, but another lesson from birthing class was about positive thinking.

I don't bother asking. Anna has spoken about twenty words total since she arrived an hour ago. She hasn't even been in the room half the time. I know all of this is intentional, because home birth is designed to foster a woman's primordial instinct and intuition. I chose it because after my scheduled C-section with Jake, without the chance to experience even one tiny contraction, I wanted to *feel* labor this time—to flow through the sensations. Also, I was kind of mad at the American medical system. After my twenty-week ultrasound, which was essentially a repeat of my experience with Jake except I was extra-super-stressed in my *advanced maternal age*, I told my midwife I wanted to try a vaginal birth after C-section (VBAC). I thought she would be thrilled. She wasn't unhappy, but it turned out there were hoops to jump through. As in, before officially making this decision, I was required by law to meet with a surgeon and sign a waiver. The form listed the risks of VBAC—mostly related to the extremely low chance that my uterine scar would rupture. At no point did he mention the risks of another surgery.

Red-faced with anger, I signed the form, left the appointment and went directly to the bookstore, where I dug out research about the risks of a repeat C-section. The list was long: infection, hemorrhage, blood clots, bowel obstruction. A few books mentioned home birth, and although this was something I'd never considered before, I found myself captivated. The more I read, the more I felt like my best chance of successfully completing a VBAC was at home, where I was comfortable and away from things that stress me out, like beeping machines, IVs, tightly closed windows, and medical personnel who are under pressure to make decisions based on money. I called Anna because she was certified to do home births, and her website said she was an engineer-turned-midwife. I appreciated this combination of hard science and homeopathy.

Chris was hesitant about home birth at first, and I couldn't blame him. One of the articles I gave him had a picture on the cover of an entire naked family in a birthing tub: mother, father and toddler. He looked up at me and frowned. "I am not doing this," he said.

I laughed. "No, no, me either."

This led to jokes about how we'd put a birthing tub in our backyard and invite the neighbors for a Happy Birthday barbecue, and they'd all drink beer and chant encouragement while I hung out in a bikini in the tub. But in all seriousness, Chris read the research and felt as compelled as I did: home birth was a safe option for us—we were only six miles from the hospital—and perfect for my personality, and Anna was a sound fit. But there was one snag. Our health insurance didn't cover home birth, so we had to pay for the whole shebang out of pocket. I decided to sell my motorcycle in order to cover the costs. It was hard to wave goodbye to my Hog, and the symbolism wasn't lost on me, but it seemed like a good trade. One adventure for another.

In my bedroom, as the pain intensifies, I think, *That was a bad trade and home birth is a stupid option*. I want my motorcycle back, and drugs–anything to ease the pain and exhaustion. I want to roll away into the night, morphing into my pre-pregnant self—Women Who Rode Away—just like the Georgia O'Keeffe poster. At the crest of a contraction, I bite my lower lip and squeeze my eyes shut, imagining that I'm riding away from childbirth. It doesn't work. My entire body tenses, all the way from my hair to my toenails. Chris kneels behind me, rubbing my back.

"Stop," I say, swatting his hand away.

Anna looks over from the edge of the room, where she is sitting on the floor, legs crossed. Her blonde hair glows in the candlelight, angelic. I can tell that she and Chris exchange some sort of glance, and it annoys me—like they're in cahoots, rolling their eyes or half-smiling or something.

"I want to go in the bathtub," I assert, bringing the attention to the level of pain I'm experiencing.

"Are you cold?" Anna asks.

"No."

Silence.

"So, can I go in the bathtub?"

"Maybe you should wait a little longer," Anna says. "It's still early."

These three words answer all of my unanswered questions. As in, I am not anywhere close to giving birth. Apparently she can tell just by looking at me.

No, I think. The clock says 11:10, which is *not early*. I would really like this to be over by midnight, because I could get a good night's sleep, our new baby in my arms, Chris by my side. I'm itching to get a start on our new life with this addition to our family.

Chris and I had stopped using condoms at the beach in Tulum, but I didn't get pregnant as quickly this time around. It didn't happen on the shores of the Caribbean, or in the few months that followed. This gave me more time to question our decision and to re-dig out my genetics textbooks and roll through the statistics in my mind, focusing on the age of my eggs. But Chris continued to cite all of the good reasons for having another baby, and I agreed with him, and we kept trying. I knew it would be nice for Jake to have a sibling, and I was excited to watch the two children interact. But I also wondered, *Would a second child be the final straw? Would we finally have to succumb to a life where outdoor adventure meant a walk to the local park?*

Eyes on the floor, I calculate how long I've been in labor: eighteen hours, technically, since 4:45 a.m., when my water broke. Chris immediately called Anna. She said something like "Oh, wonderful! Why don't you try to get a little more sleep?"

I snorted. I mean, honestly. Does anyone go back to sleep once they realize, *I'm having a baby today!*

Well, Anna certainly had a point, and I wish I'd listened to her advice, because now it's almost *tomorrow*—the longest I've ever been immersed in any physically taxing event. The closest things I can think of are my twelve-hour summit of Long's Peak, or the time I biked 500 miles from Minneapolis to Chicago. Neither were anything like this.

So anyway, I want to speed things up. I consider how to do this and decide my best option is to push forward, just like I would if I were on a long distance bike ride or hike.

I decide to trump Anna. "I want to go in the bath," I assert. Strategically, I'm thinking this will relax my muscles and coerce them into dropping the baby magically on the floor. Some women report that this happens—that their baby just falls out—and I don't see why this can't be my reality, too.

"Okay," says Anna, shrugging. She nods at Chris. "Let's do a bath."

Chris looks at me. "Are you sure?" he asks.

"Yes." He doesn't question me further. Chris has seen me in lots of intense athletic situations, competing in triathlons, mountain biking steep fire roads, portaging a canoe in the Boundary Waters, and he knows I often don't like to talk. He pulls me up and leads me to the bathroom, and runs the water while I dump myself into the gray basin, which we scrubbed clean a couple of days ago. I forget to take off my tank top and underwear.

Initially, the warm water feels good, lapping against my back and belly, and I think, *See, I am going to rock this thing out!* But then another contraction comes, a mountain of searing pain, and everything in the bathtub begins to irritate me: the smell of the water, the moist air above the water, the water touching my skin, the hard porcelain under my huge-feeling ass. I pound my fists against the edge of the tub, my entire body tense as my abdomen squeezes so tight, for so long, that it takes my breath away.

When it's over, Chris looks at me with soft eyes. "I wish I could help you," he says.

"You can't."

"You're amazing."

I half smile.

He shakes his head. "Good thing Jake isn't here."

I puff air out of my mouth in agreement. We'd entertained the idea of having Jake present at the birth, so he could see his sibling emerge into the world, prompted by a video we watched that made home birth seem much more tranquil than this. But now, as I writhe and whine, overpowering the soothing music, practically dousing the candle flames with my carrying on, I realize it would've freaked Jake out to see me like this. It might've traumatized him, providing yet another bullet to the list of ways a parent can mess their kid up for life, turning him into a co-dependent addict, or a serial killer.

"I love you," says Chris.

Another contraction begins. "No," I say. I can't believe it. I barely got a break. "No, no, no!" I shout. I look wide-eyed at Chris and tense through the horrendous cramping sensation—by far the strongest yet—pounding the tub, kicking my legs, pulling at my hair, holding my breath. When it's over, after what feels like ten hours, I stand up. "Get me out of here," I say. "This isn't working! The tub is stupid! Hurry! Before another one comes!"

Anna and Chris both rush to my side, and there is a flurry of activity as they peel off my wet clothes and towel me off. I barely even notice them because I'm consumed with my pain, chest heaving, teeth clenched, looking wildly around the room for anything that might make me feel better. Maybe I could sit in the shower? Lean against the bed frame? What did they say in the birthing class? Breathe? Well, I am beyond breathing. We should just go to the hospital. I need the hospital! I shiver uncontrollably.

Chris hugs me from behind and Anna holds a small bottle up to my face. "Carrie," she demands. "Stick out your tongue. Let's try this. It's a natural calming agent."

I scoff. "I don't want natural! I want morphine!" But I stick out my tongue, hoping Anna will surprise me with some organic plant-derived remedy that's actually effective.

Chris leads me back into the bedroom, somehow supporting most of my enormous weight with his arms. The clock says 12:30; it's now the next day. *This is eternal.* I collapse face-down on the mattress we placed on the floor, my chest elevated on a pile of pillows. I don't feel calm *at all*. Tears fill my eyes and I can't stop them. They rush down my face and the room goes blank. Before I know it I am wailing, hugging the pillows with my arms, face smashed against the blue linens.

"Carrie." Anna's voice, steady and strong, comes from behind me. "What do you need right now?"

I sob louder.

"What do you need to do?" she repeats.

I push my face up. "I don't want to do this anymore!" I scream. "I can't!" I repeat this over and over into oblivion, until all I can hear is my own voice in my head–desperate, exhausted. Terrified. For the first time in my life, I recognize that what I am experiencing is pure, raw fear. This is as far out of my comfort zone as I've ever been. I wasn't scared in a torrential downpour while backpacking in the Porcupine Mountains in Michigan, or when I pedaled 100 miles a day for five days. It never occurred to me that I wouldn't finish the summit of Long's Peak. But this? Motherhood? Childbirth? *I don't know how I am going to make it.*

Anna appears at the front of the mattress. She squats down in front of me, right at my level, like a sports coach. Her face is six inches from my own. She tilts my chin up and breathes deeply. "Carrie, you wanted this," she states.

I sob, snot dripping all over her hand and the pillows. "I didn't."

"Carrie, you did."

"I did not!"

"You chose this."

I look away, sniffling. *I hate her.*

Another contraction starts, and I bow down in front of Anna, screaming and crying. The exertion leaves me listless, and when the wave of pain diminishes, I just continue to lay there, forehead on the pillow. Sweat trickles down my back. My throat feels dry. I breathe my own breath against the cotton pillowcase. I don't look at Anna. I don't, because I know she's right.

In this position of complete submission, I concede. I squeeze my eyes shut and admit that I wanted this. I chose this. I opted for home birth.

I just didn't think it would be this hard. When I was pregnant, I scoffed at the stories of three-day labors and mind-blowing pain. I reverted to my old way of thinking, when I was pregnant with Jake. I thought, *Lots of women have babies. It can't possibly be that hard.* Now I'm embarrassed. I was so arrogant.

I slowly lift my head. I look at Anna. "Fuck," I say.

She purses her lips and nods, knowingly. She has two children of her own.

I bite my bottom lip.

"Isn't it amazing there are so many *people*?" she asks.

This makes me smile, and then laugh. Anna joins me, and the room fills with our deep, darkly comical giggles. "Fuck, fuck, fuck!" I say.

My abdomen grips, and I stop laughing and cursing.

Anna nods. "Now, Carrie," she says. "What do you need to do?"

As the gripping intensifies, a light bulb flashes in my mind. I realize she is intentionally not using the word "think."

This is not about what *I think* I need to do, but what *I know*. I need to dig deeper, to find what exists deep down in that place that only women possess.

I close my eyes and let go. I surrender. For a reason I can't pinpoint, I find myself moving into a modified position I know from yoga—Child's Pose—with my chest and shoulders resting higher on the pillows, and my lower back on the bed. The pain doesn't stop. It doesn't lessen. In fact, the contractions get stronger—one on top of the other—like I am constantly being washed out to sea and grasped by huge swells and tossed around in the dizzying chaos, unsure which way is up. But now I focus on relaxing the muscles that don't need to work: my arms, shoulders, lower thighs. I look to my core. I moan without inhibition, a deep lowing that sounds primal and eerie. In this place, time stops. The candles flicker. I don't think one single thought. Later, Chris described my eyes as trance-like, faraway.

In the hazy light of dawn, I finally cross the finish line. I give birth to a dark-haired baby girl. She's perfect, with pink skin and blue eyes, and she lets out a few cries and then snuggles immediately into my chest, latching onto my breast. I kiss her on the head, nose, fingers.

After she's finished nursing, Anna takes her for a moment to record APGAR scores. I barely even remember to wonder if everything's okay, because I am physically exhausted and detached from my thinking mind. I imagine the joys of raising a girl with her brother looking on protectively. In my hormone-buzzed mind everything is watery and soft and perfect. I see yellow sundresses and blue hiking boots and dancing on the beach with my very own daughter.

"Congratulations," says Anna. She records the time of birth as 4:58 a.m., almost exactly twenty-four hours after the wheels set into motion. "You did great," she says. "That was a textbook birth."

I roll my eyes. "Yeah, right."

She smirks. "Really."

"You're just being nice." I think about how nothing in my life has been textbook, yet somehow this has.

Chris sits down on the bed. I look at him like I haven't seen him in days. His eyes are bloodshot and dark-rimmed, like he is drunk, or high, or both. But he's glowing. "Hey," I say.

"Hey, honey." He beams.

"Thank you for staying up all night with me."

He kisses me lightly on the cheek. He tears up.

We look at our baby girl together, noting her minuscule fingernails and precious ears. She sticks out her tongue, a trait that will follow her into childhood, and we giggle. We try a few names out on her, from a list we made: Leah, Julia, and Elise, but we don't make a decision.

And then I close my eyes, unable to stay awake any longer. "That was hard," I say.

Chris touches his hand to my cheek. "You are my hero."

Maybe it's cliché. Maybe it's sappy. But I don't care. I feel like I conquered the biggest summit of all time: my own mind. I feel exactly like a hero.

11

Superhero

Three Years, One Month into Motherhood

It's mid-morning on a Tuesday, and everything should be great, really, because it's summer in Northern Colorado, and I live in a lovely place to raise my two children. I am now a mother of *two* children! Birds chirp. The sun shines. Scattered blooms accent our yard—patches of Snow-on-the-Mountain and Verbena and Monkshood—the result of Chris's close-to-home landscaping talent. Across the street, my neighbors' horses and donkeys and randomly rescued peacocks wander around a pasture that overlooks the foothills, and if I listen closely, I can hear the rush of the Poudre River. The whole scene looks like a Colorado calendar. $14.95 for most people. Free for me.

I inhale and wipe a dab of crust out of the corner of my eye. I haven't looked in the mirror yet today, but I'm guessing I look skinny. Skinnier than yesterday, for sure. Since I gave birth to Elise a month ago, my tummy has been deflating in regular increments, like a balloon losing air, and my maternity shirts have become long and baggy and wonderfully too big.

Chris jokingly says to me each morning, "Carrie, you are half the woman you were yesterday."

We giggle and hug and he goes to work. This time, Chris took three weeks of paternity leave, one more week than when Jake was born. A few years later, nothing has changed with America's maternity and paternity leave policies—there's still no national policy mandating paid leave—so his time off was unpaid. As a freelancer, I didn't exactly take leave, but I met some deadlines in advance and arranged for a lighter load for a few months.

This morning, I have just put Elise down for a nap in the upstairs bedroom where she typically sleeps for hours on end, arms overhead, in a bassinet attached to our bed. No swings or swaddles necessary for this kid, unlike her discerning brother, discovered by trial and error, changing things up just enough to adequately confuse her parents who thought they'd mastered the Happy Baby thing. That's why we named her Elise. It seemed to fit her peaceful-independent-free nature.

Jake plays on the living room floor with a smattering of toy cars and a ramp he created out of shoeboxes. He crashes each car off the edge of the boxes in a suicidal mission, and then laughs when they land on their sides, or overturn completely. His Y-chromosome is still raging. Lately, he's begun turning sticks into guns, a jaw-dropping development, considering we don't own a gun, and he only watches TV shows like *Sesame Street* and *Bob the Builder*, where I'm pretty sure they're singing the ABC's and not introducing kids to weapons. I hate watching kids' shows, with puppets singing and playing banjos, and animated construction vehicles navigating new (except almost exactly the same) crises every day, but I might have to monitor more closely, in case Jake's magically figured out how to use the remote control and is using his miniature thumbs to turn the channel to *MacGyver* re-runs. More likely, it's a result of his Y-chromosome. Where was that in my genetics textbook?

I lean against the kitchen counter and pop a pill into my mouth. It goes down easy. No dig-in-my-heels resistance to anti-depressants this time around. My home birth midwife is not the one who recommended them (I mean, she gave me a flower remedy instead of morphine during Elise's birth), but our pediatrician, who is also our family doctor, suggested I start on a low dose of Zoloft right away to prevent any possible postpartum depression. I did not argue. I'd take my medication this time, just like the doctor ordered, butchering up the pills, and I'd adjust to life with two children and embrace my beautiful yard. Look how well things are going! It's Snuggle fabric softener, supersized.

I place a mug of water in the microwave to make herbal tea, because I'm still trying to kick my caffeine addiction, although if today is like every other day, I'll break down and drink a diet soda by noon. Out the back window I see my neighbor, George, lumbering out of his house toward his detached garage-turned-taxidermy-studio. He's wearing dusty jeans and a brown T-shirt and he strokes his white beard with one hand, carrying a rack of antlers with the other.

"Ugh," I say. We share a gravel driveway with George and his wife and their grown son, yet we have almost nothing in common. They snowmobile; we snowshoe. They trap animals for pelts; we support conservation organizations. They gamble; we save. They're very nice people—we often exchange pleasantries, and I respect their views. My own father hunted when I was a kid, and I understand the benefits of filling your freezer with meat. It's just that if we ever had an in-depth conversation with George and his wife about anything, we'd probably agree on almost nothing, which goes both ways. (Imagine if we'd invited them to our outdoor Happy Birthday home birth barbeque!)

George enters his studio, which has a sign on the door that says "WELKOME." I don't see what's welcoming about the glazed-over eyes of a stuffed elk head. I've never been inside, but Chris tells me there are a dozen or so animals: deer, fish, pronghorn antelope. Even a mountain lion. People in pickup trucks pull into our driveway many days each week—especially during prime hunting season—and unload their kills, dead animals that they want to preserve forever on their fireplace mantels. One day, two men lugged a black bear inside, loosely wrapped in a garbage bag. Another day, a bobcat.

The microwave beeps and I gladly turn from the window. Tossing a chamomile tea bag into my mug, I glance in at Jake, who is pretending his fingers are police officers rushing to the scene of a major car accident. There's always a problem, and he saves the day.

A high-pitched sound startles me. I freeze. *What's that?*

It sounds like it's coming from the upstairs bedroom. Since becoming a mother for the second time, I've re-acquired the superpowers I remember gaining when Jake was a newborn. Especially ultra-sensitive hearing, like a (live) moose or elk. One time, days after Elise was born and I'd dashed to Walmart for a few We Need items, déjà vu from when Jake was a newborn except there was parking, I swore I heard Elise crying at home while I was standing in the cereal aisle. I called Chris, and he confirmed she was fussy.

I creep toward the stairs and perk up my ears. The noise isn't human. It sounds like the ring of my cell phone. *What? Is my phone up there? Did I leave it?*

Damn! Silently berating myself, I tiptoe up the stairs, crossing my fingers that Elise will manage, out of some great stroke of luck, to sleep through the ringing. But when I'm on the third step from the top, she begins crying. It starts as a slow whimper, builds momentum, and progresses into a full-out wail. I imagine her red face and tangled blanket and flailing limbs. I set my mug on the step and grab at the doorknob.

The doorknob doesn't turn. "Fuck," I whisper. I jiggle the brass handle. No luck. I begin turning it wildly, and kicking the wood with my toe. "What the hell?"

Oh no. My breath catches in my chest. *It's locked.*

I run my fingers through my hair, but they get stuck in a knot that I didn't know was there. I push and pull and wiggle the knob, and I pound at the door. How did I manage to lock my baby, and my cell phone, in my bedroom? How could I do this? My mother would be appalled. Social services would lock me up. I think of the time I dropped Jake on the hot pavement outside my non-profit office. And now this: another scenario that's not anywhere on the list of "50 Ways Your Baby Might Die." Why do I keep adding bullets to the list?

I stand there, stunned, as Elise sobs. My hands tremble. There are only a couple of inches of wood separating me from my newborn, but I might as well be miles away. My nerves feel frazzled, as if their protective sheath has melted away, leaving them raw and exposed. Biting my bottom lip, I realize I feel as helpless as my own child.

Jake peeks his head into the stairwell, eyebrows furrowed. "Mommy," he says. "Go get her."

"I can't! She's locked in!"

His blue eyes get huge. "Uh oh."

"It's okay," I breathe. "Just keep playing."

He stands there, looking worried.

Options swirl like a tornado in my mind. How can I solve this? I could kick in the door. Get a ladder and go in through the open window, which is the only other way into this room, or call Chris or the police. But wait, I don't have a phone, because we don't have a land line anymore. And where do we store our ladder? If I try to kick in the door (I imagine a series of less-than-graceful karate kicks), Jake and Elise will freak out in the commotion.

Then I remember the fire station. It's only a half mile away—a one-minute drive. Firefighters save kittens from trees. Certainly they can help rescue my baby.

I scramble down the stairs, almost tripping and falling, and scoop Jake into my arms. "Car ride," I say.

He smiles. "Car car!" His bare feet dangle from my arms.

In the driveway, I glance up at the window to the bedroom. Elise's wails pierce the soft air. I try to slow my breath. She's not going to die, I tell myself. She's safe in her bassinet. *But what if she gets tangled in her blanket? What if she works herself into a corner and suffocates? What if she feels abandoned and this incident scars her for life?*

As I open the car door, I catch my reflection in the window. My hair looks like a lion's mane, and there's a dollop of something brown on my cheek. Wet spots swell over my nipples.

The skin under my eyes sags, and there's a scratch on my neck. I look like I've been living in a dark closet for days with no food or water. I had no idea. I thought I was doing fine.

A gruff voice says, "You okay?"

I spin around. It's George. "Oh, hi." I cross my arms over my chest.

"You seem panicked." He wipes his hand on his jeans. His belly strains against his T-shirt.

"Um." I keep one arm over my chest and smooth my hair with my other hand. "It's Elise." I clear my throat. "She's locked in the upstairs bedroom."

He raises his eyebrows. "Is the window open?"

I nod.

In one second flat, he springs into action. Even overweight, he moves more gracefully than I do at this point, and in several quick motions, he disappears into the taxidermy studio, comes out with a ladder, and hauls it through the gate to my house. Placing the ladder under the window, he climbs the rungs, looking like Santa on a summer delivery. At the window, he stops, tears off the screen and hoists himself through the window. Jake and I watch from the lawn, jaws dropped.

"Wow!" exclaims Jake. "Superman!"

Suddenly I feel heavy, like a brick of fatigue has settled onto my shoulders—cumulative weight from the last weeks, when my number of children doubled, and the responsibility seemed to quadruple, and I was measuring my well-being by how loose my maternity shirts were feeling each morning.

George peers out the window. "Are you coming up?"

"Oh! Yes." It reminds me of when Jake was born, when I was

gazing at him in the mirrored lamp and the doctor said, "Look at your baby!"

I fly into the house, stumble up the stairs, and enter the room. George is standing over Elise, cooing. She grasps his thumb in her fingers. Her face is pink and her cheeks are wet, but she looks content there with George. For a second, I stand still, watching this moment of unclouded adoration.

Then I pick up Elise and pull her into my arms. "Honey, I'm sorry."

Eyes on the ground, George steps back. As I snuggle with Elise, cooing and apologizing profusely, I glance around the room and take in the surroundings: breast pump, maxi pads, journal, diapers, pink and yellow onesies. It looks like a hurricane came through and left a pile of debris that screams "Motherhood!" This space must feel as foreign to George as his taxidermy studio does to me.

I look up at George. "Thank you," I say.

"No problem."

I feel my face reddening. "I can't believe I did that. I'm so embarrassed."

George looks down the stairs, watches Jake clamber up. "Well, you've got your hands full."

I nod. "Some days it's a lot." Really, it feels more like a *ton*. Like a gargantuan responsibility. When Chris leaves for work each morning, my heart secretly sinks. On the surface, we giggle. I put on my mask. We joke about my deflating belly. I pretend that I'm fine. I take my Zoloft and focus on my pretty yard and my herbal tea. But there are a lot of things that are complicated: managing two nap schedules, checking email in the thirty-minute increment when the kids' naps overlap, reading to Jake while I nurse Elise, changing what feels like millions of diapers (my two kids alone could seemingly fill an entire landfill). And then I've somehow managed to contract the painful breast infection mastitis not only once, but twice, in Elise's short life, requiring antibiotics and hot compresses and pain medication.

I try hard not to focus on these challenges, or get caught up in the minutia of mothering, because every job has important parts that aren't pleasant. But because things like diapering just don't make me feel fulfilled, I need to have balance, and I'm off course in that area. Is anything less than total immersion in domesticity possible right now? Is there any other choice?

George touches my elbow. The warmth of his fingers makes my shoulders soften. For the first time, I realize his eyes are a gentle blue.

The color reminds me of the time I went swimming with Chris in the Caribbean in Tulum, which makes me remember our adventure list. It got stuffed away before Elise was born, again, when we were cleaning out a space for her crib, and I wonder where it is: in a box in the downstairs closet? Maybe this would be a good time to pull it out. It might help just to look at it, to see what things we've managed to accomplish. To peruse my list of motherhood milestones. And perhaps to see what lies ahead. I know Europe is still on there, and rural Mexico. And maybe I'll add to it–activities that aren't so big and time consuming, that I could manage now, while I'm in the thick of things: hiking, camping, a one-day writing conference, or a family road trip. Plus, I don't always have to be *on a trip* to be happy—sometimes the mere act of planning the trip is enough: Tracking airfares on Kayak.com. Reading a magazine story about an adventurous family who's living in Patagonia. Looking at a world map. Flipping through a guidebook in the library that offers tips for visiting a new place. I make a mental note to turn on a Kayak flight alert for somewhere (anywhere), just so I'll get those emails in my inbox every day. Which will remind me that I will, at some point, buy another plane ticket to somewhere.

I think of my friend who's living in Central America right now with her two school-aged daughters. She began planning the trip when her kids were very young, starting by envisioning the adventure, and then doing some long-term planning, because she knew finances were going to be an important consideration. She says if she hadn't done that, given herself lots of time, everyday life would've taken over and the "heart stuff," the things that take her out of her home and away from all the responsibilities and back to that place where she feels fully herself, couldn't happen. She ended up finding a perfect adventure at a sustainable farm in Costa Rica.

I can do that. I can dig out our adventure list and begin to envision our next trip, and then take steps toward making it happen. That will serve as my balance right now.

Jake appears in the doorway. "Elise!" he exclaims. He grabs at her feet. George raises his hand and gives him a high-five.

"Hey Jake," he says. "Wanna help me pack up the ladder?"

Jake jumps up and down. "Yes." It's Bob the Builder in real life.

George looks at me. "Okay?"

I nod, thrilled to have a few moments alone with Elise, and grateful for George's ability to understand that. Thankful that he inspired this insightful moment where I brought myself back to center.

I stand in the upstairs window, rocking Elise, watching George collapse his ladder and haul it back to the studio. Jake babbles at his side, hands gesturing wildly, undoubtedly recounting the whole rescue scenario. I hold Elise up to the window, aiming her eyes toward George. I know she's too young to see him, but maybe it's not about age. I didn't really see George until a few moments ago. "That's a real life superhero," I say.

As George and Jake enter the door that says, "WELKOME," I think about how maybe, just maybe, I'll venture down to the taxidermy studio someday and ask George to give me a tour. Certainly that would be an adventure of its own; a walk into a world that is different from mine, even though it is only steps away. It would strengthen this bridge George and I just built, instead of widening the canyon. Mentally I add George, my next door neighbor, to my global community, the list of people who have touched me, and taught me.

12

Unwanted Passenger

Three and a Half Years into Motherhood

I wake up at dawn in the desert. The walls of my tent rustle in the breeze, and my breath swirls up from my mouth. Pulling my knit hat over my ears, I look out the window and glare through the scrubby pine at the campsite next to me, which contains a smattering of coolers and a tent that's as big as an RV. Last night, their cadre of children shrieked into the darkness for hours, playing a game that involved loud thumping noises, like horseshoes or croquet.

My children are at home in Colorado with Chris. I came here for an uninterrupted night of red dirt and full moon; to lie on my back, listening to my heartbeat in my chest, breathing the rich aroma of earth and air and sky. Except it's more than that. I'm here because I'm scared. Actually, I'm Really Fucking Terrified. What's bothering me might be nothing, or it might be *something*, and I want to know which it is.

At six months old, Elise is skinny. Born a healthy seven pounds, she hasn't gained much in her newborn months, and she's struggled with constipation. At her three-month well check, her weight didn't even make the growth chart. Which is not what people mean when they use the phrase "off the charts." It's the opposite. Scientifically speaking, it might mean "failure to thrive," a term that sounds hopeless and could indicate a whole host of disorders. But our pediatrician, who is very intelligent and compassionate, and aware of my education, said at the three-month visit, "Let's just keep watching this." I've been unable to stop staring at the medical charts, and my daughter.

My stomach growls and I zip myself out of my tent. I stand on soft sand. Stretching my arms overhead, and twisting my achy hips from sleeping on my side, I look all around. The campsites are dead silent, still. It looks like the beginning of a horror movie, when everything appears peaceful, and then suddenly it's not. Everyone is sleeping, curled up in their tents, snuggled together, recovering after their raucous night, and then...

"Car camping," I mutter, changing the subject in my mind. I notice that all of the sites around me are cluttered with *stuff*, from awnings to propane cook stoves to oversized lawn chairs. One group has pink flamingo lawn ornaments stuck in the sand. Another has seven bikes. In contrast, I have one tent and a fold-up camp chair. Even though I can't see any people, I know this place is teeming with them. Since I'm the first one up and last night was not peaceful, I decide to get a head start on the hiking trail to Delicate Arch, ahead of the crowd, where I can be alone like I want to.

No one I know goes on solo camping trips to deal with fear, for obvious reasons. Camping itself is scary. There are wild animals and weird noises. All of this feels scarier alone. But for me, it works well. I guess it's my version of "retail therapy," accomplishing the same sense of (temporary) escape from one's worries. I pour myself into survival mode and it's hard to think about anything else. Usually I take trips that involve backpacking into the mountains, where I don't have to share my experience, carrying everything I need, and a few things I want, on my back. Last month, I hauled a forty-pound pack up to 8,500 feet elevation in the Roosevelt National Forest in Northern Colorado, pitched my tent, hung my food bag from a rope in a tree, and reveled in silence for two days. It was a quick overnight—I'd just finished breastfeeding, so it was also a celebration of sorts. Solitude is my favorite meditation.

Lately, I'd been reading Edward Abbey's *The Journey Home*, and his descriptions of "The Great American Desert" made me want to experience first-hand the simple lines and curves of stone and shrub. I had no experience in desert terrain, so it seemed that a good first trip would be car camping in Arches National Park near Moab, Utah. It would be Desert 101. Desert for Dummies. I timed the trip for the day after Elise's six-month doctor appointment, because I knew I'd welcome the opportunity to be alone afterwards—to celebrate or worry. If the news was ambiguous or bad, I could sit and pick at the loose threads on my tent all alone, without anyone telling me to "Try to think about something else," or "It's going to be okay."

Elise eats well. She has energy. She smiles and coos. She gets bored easily at home, so I pedal her everywhere in the bike trailer when Jake is at daycare and Chris is at work. We go to the library for story time. To the park, where she wants to swing all day, arms in the air. Sometimes we sit by the river, just the two of us, throwing rocks and eating cookies and juice for lunch. I see myself in her wild spirit and daydream about girls' trips when she's older. We'll go to the beach and dance in the sand, or visit art museums in Italy and eat pizza and drink hand-squeezed lemonade. Maybe I'll take her to Bali, where we'll ride motorcycles and go surfing.

It's just that Elise is waif-like and not shaped like the bell curve she's supposed to be following. I've been asked a zillion questions about her eating habits, bowel movements, and poop color, not just by the doctor, but by well-meaning acquaintances, too. Feeling scrutinized, and needing someone to blame, I've chosen America. I sit around, stewing, thinking irrational thoughts like, *Doesn't our culture value thinness? If I had a fat baby, people would compliment me on her chubby cheeks and pudgy arms, but obesity is an epidemic in America! Why do we value fat babies and thin adults? The growth charts in America are the root of the problem!*

On the morning of Elise's six-month appointment, I fed her three times: Puréed squash. Cheerios. Smashed pears.

———

I toss my knife, which is my companion on solo trips, into my sedan, and glance at myself in the rearview mirror. My hair poofs out from under my hat—clown-like—and I comb it down with my fingers. There are dark circles under my eyes, and I notice that the large blotches of hyperpigmentation on my face that started with Jake's birth and won't go away, look even darker and more unsightly than usual. Big, brown, serrated stars on my cheeks and forehead that make me feel very self-conscious, partly because people mention it often. Just last week I was at the grocery store and a woman approached me. "I used to have that *problem* with my face," she said, pointing to my cheek, and then suggesting a skin care product.

I frown, wishing I hadn't looked in the mirror. Slamming the door and walking to the back of my car, I open my trunk to grab breakfast–a peanut butter granola bar from my cloth food bag. But as I pull my hand out of the bag, something moves inside the trunk. I freeze. Beady black eyes stare at me, and tiny feet grasp the upholstery. I jump back. *What is that?*

The creature darts right and left, its gray fur a haze. "Mouse!" I exclaim. I grab a stick from the ground, like I would if encountering a bear or a mountain lion. Our movements mirror each other: wide-eyed, quick, agitated. He disappears behind the lining of my trunk. "Shit," I say.

I step back and sigh. I consider whether I classify "mouse in my trunk" as a big deal or a minor inconvenience. When I was planning this trip, I referenced Abbey's long list of potential desert hazards: rattlesnakes, scorpions, conenose kissing bugs, black widows. But his sarcasm downplayed the danger, and I decided I'd do what I always do in the outdoors: keep my eyes open.

———

Two days ago, on the baby scale in the doctor's office, Elise was crying so hard her eyes were closed. I tried to wrap a blanket around her naked body, to protect her from the cold metal, but the nurse gently pulled it off and handed it to me.

Desperate for the highest possible reading, I kept prodding Elise into the middle of the scale, making sure there wasn't a stray limb touching the counter. "Sit still!" I scolded.

The nurse patted my arm. "I got what I need," she said. "I'll be right back."

When she returned with the printout, I was rocking Elise in my arms, holding her tight in her blanket. I grabbed the paper and scanned the chart wildly for the dot representing my daughter. *Where was it?* It was at the very bottom of the page. Somewhere between zero and the first percentile. *Okay,* I thought, *she's on the chart.* The pediatrician walked in then and began the routine exam, listening to Elise's heart and lungs and asking me the questions she is required to ask. I started to breathe freely because she was smiling, and smiling means good news, right?

Then she went over to the growth chart to peruse it. I held my breath. Time stopped. She looked up. "I think we should repeat Elise's newborn screen," she said.

I balked. "What?"

"I think she's fine. I just want to make sure."

"What are you concerned about?"

"I really think she's fine. Let's just double check."

I couldn't get her to say anything out loud, but I knew she was thinking *something.* She was trying to protect me from my own brain. But I know. I know the newborn screen is a blood test that detects a litany of conditions. Some of these conditions are serious metabolic disorders, the names barely pronounceable—Phenylketonuria, Galactosemia—which would indicate that Elise is, in fact, not thriving normally. Metabolic pathways run the entire body, and when a mutation blocks them from creating healthy tissues, excess nutrients can build up and cause brain damage. And then there's cystic fibrosis. And other disorders I've managed to forget. I would love Elise the same if she were afflicted with any of these disorders. But what about the worst? The unthinkable?

Because it was Friday afternoon, the nurse sent us immediately to the lab at the hospital to do the test before the weekend. They would have the results early the following week. I demanded to know *which* day early next week. Monday, they said, or Tuesday. I dragged Jake by the arm and held Elise tightly, leaving Chris message after message on his cell phone. "Please meet us," I said. "I need you."

———

Today in the desert, I wish Chris were here, once again, to help me deal with this mouse. The rodent that outsmarted my keen eyes. But I chose this: to be alone with my worries, my fears, the unexpected. Abbey would laugh at the mouse, but I'm only half-smiling. *What if the mouse gets into the car and crawls up my pant leg while I'm driving? What if it bites me? What if causes me to veer off the road into a ditch?*

A man from the neighboring campsite walks by. He brushes dark wisps from his eyes. "Morning," he says.

I wave with my stick.

He smiles. "Why are you wielding a stick?"

I point at my trunk. "Mouse."

He squints.

"Mouse!" I repeat.

"Really?"

I nod.

He sidles up to my trunk and smiles. "Unwanted passenger, huh?"

I would like to laugh, but I don't.

The man peers closer. "Do you have food in there?"

"Yeah."

He rummages around and pulls out a Ziploc bag of Corn Nuts, which has a hole chewed in the corner. "Culprit," he says.

"Oh."

"You gotta keep food sealed."

I blush. I glance at his coolers.

"It's probably harmless," he says. "Unless it poops all over and you get hantavirus."

He says this half-jokingly, but I suck in my breath. Isn't that deadly, or at least medically serious? What do I even know about hantavirus? I think it's rare, but I also know that my brother-in-law wears a mask when he sweeps out his garage, for protection. And I've seen brochures by the Centers for Disease Control warning campers about the dangers. I transport my children in this car.

Danger! I think. *Danger!* Maybe I'm over-reacting, but I can't help it. I love my children so much. I love listening to the patter of their feet. I love Elise's buttery skin. I love watching Jake watch his little sister. I had no idea I could love anything this much—it's just like I anticipated way back in graduate school—and I'm not willing to take any risks.

In the waiting room of the hospital, I held my children close. I bounced Elise in my lap while Jake snuggled into my side, watching TV. The receptionist gave me a heating pad to warm Elise's foot.

"A heel stick will be much less traumatic for her," she said. We waited like that for an hour, until the pad was cold. Chris hadn't called back—he was probably stuck in meetings, not even aware of my frantic messages.

Finally, the technician called. "Elise!"

Leading us back to the line of cubby-holed rooms, she glanced at Elise's heel. "We can't do a heel stick," she said.

"They recommended a heel stick at reception because it would be less traumatic," I said. "They *gave* me this heating pad."

"Well, she's too old."

I held up Elise's arm. "Do you see the size of her arm? It's stick-like. How are you going to find a vein?"

She frowned. "It's going to be tough. But we can't do the heel stick."

It took two of us—me and an intern—to hold Elise down on an adult-sized table while the tech tied a rubber cord around her arm. Elise wailed. I sniffled. Jake tugged at my leg, looking up at me with concerned eyes. "Mommy, is she okay?" he kept asking. I had no hands to comfort him with.

It took three needle sticks to find a decent vein and the tech filled two large vials with more blood than I knew existed in Elise's entire body. The skin on her upper arm turned immediately purple, a bruise the size of a half dollar. I held Elise close. "I'm sorry," I said.

———

At the campground, with my stick, I tap all around the inside of my trunk. I tap harder. I pound. "Dammit mouse," I say. "Get out here."

The man shrugs. "I'd get a trap and lure him with bread."

I envision the scenario: Driving twenty miles into Moab to the hardware store, buying a trap, sitting on the curb, waiting for the thud, holding the dead mouse by its tail and tossing it in a garbage can. It makes my stomach turn. I don't want to drive all those miles. I want the mouse out now.

"Thanks for your help," I say to my neighbor, waving him away. "I'll figure this out."

"Alrighty. Good luck." He trudges away, waving to a young woman who's sliding out of her tent, bundled in fleece.

Furious, I swipe at the trunk with the stick, poking it in every crevice I can find. Then I throw the stick to the ground, tearing at the inner lining with my hands. *Where is the mouse?* I'm sure I look wild, crazy, like the psychotic killer who's come to hack up the campground. But I don't care. I rip and tear and pound.

The mouse does not come out, apparently hidden in a safe spot, and I jut my hips out behind me and lean into the trunk, placing my head in my hands. "Fuck," I whisper, "This is so fucking unfair."

And then I think, *Leave my children alone*, which is really what I mean. Motherhood has awakened in me emotions that run deeper than the sand under my feet, than the age-old roots that tether the trees to the earth, making me fiercely protective, my guard high at all times. I realize I'm using the stick to pound out not only the mouse, but every danger that faces my kids. I want to keep them safe at all costs, and I hate that I can't. There are car accidents and kidnappers and school shootings. Whether it's a secret residing in their genetic code, or the rare possibility of a deadly virus, there is so much that is out of my control. And yet, I feel that it is my job to protect. Isn't that the pact one makes in becoming a parent? *I am your mother and I promise to keep you safe.*

Exhausted, I collapse onto the ground and sit with my head against the bumper of my trunk. I close my eyes. I think: *I miss the days when I didn't love anything this much.* When I lived for myself. When I didn't have to worry about lives other than my own.

But of course, I wouldn't trade my children for a less worrisome life. And I realize that maybe I need to revise the pact, just like I revised the fantasy of my life as a mom. Maybe the pact should say, *I am your mother and I will do everything I can to protect you.* Maybe I need to accept this.

Elise's blood test is out of my hands. Her fate is not my decision. But here in the desert, with a mouse in my trunk, I have control. I can take action. And right now that feels good—to be able to do something. With a plan, I can return the mouse to his habitat and remove any remote risk to my family. And obviously, this is not going to happen by pounding the living shit out of my car. The only thing I've done is terrified the creature into hiding from the psychotic killer in his own personal horror movie.

I try to think like a mouse. What would he want? I believe the answer is food, freedom. He wants to survive just like I do. So I empty the contents out of my trunk, place a pile of Corn Nuts in the center, leave the trunk lid open, and walk toward the fire pit. I look back every ten seconds, as if I'm going to magically see a mouse flying Superman-style out of my trunk, holding a corn nut in its mouth. *Not realistic.*

Then, an epiphany. I walk back to my trunk, *remove* the Corn Nuts, put them in my pocket and leave the scene. I give him space to crawl out, so he realizes there's nothing for him in my car, so he will go searching for his own food on the desert floor.

I climb up a wall of slickrock at the edge of my campsite and sit on the smooth, rusty bed. It is perfectly silent. Red sand sifts through my fingers. The air smells like earth. I look up. A smear of moon dots the indigo sky, and in the distance, an arch of sandstone curves up from green pines. The contrast of colors and textures is stunning, and I realize that this is it, my moment of peaceful desert immersion. It's the best I'm going to get on this trip. I recline on my elbows and close my eyes and breathe.

Two days later, on Tuesday, I'm at home holding Elise on my hip when the phone rings. The morning is chilly, but the sky is the same azure I remember from Utah. The mouse is long gone; I never saw him again. I look at the number on my cell phone—it's the clinic.

I pick up the phone tentatively. "Hello?"

"Is this Carrie?" the nurse asks.

"Uh huh."

"I have the results of Elise's screen."

"Okay." I grip Elise tighter.

The next moments are a blur. The nurse says all kinds of words, syllables that run together like watercolors. But then she says something I hear clearly: Normal. She says everything looks normal. *Elise's results are within normal limits.*

"Yes!" I say. "Thank you! Thank you so much!"

"I'm glad to ease your mind," she says, and I know she really means this, because I remember how desperately I wanted to give good news to parents in the genetics clinic when I was a student.

I smile at Elise. She smiles back, blissfully naïve. I hang up the phone and hug her. I close my eyes tight for a second, to capture this moment in my mind, before we resume living our ever-changing lives.

13

Wild Mama

Four Years into Motherhood

I dislike the following terms: play date, kiddo, binky. Also, when parents share their toddlers' ages in months. When I take Jake and Elise, roughly four and two, to the playground, I set them free in the sand, sit in a corner with a book, and watch parents follow their kids around. Every once in a while I get up to push Elise in a swing. At all costs, I avoid adult eye contact, because I don't want to join a conversation about sleep training, potty training, or minivans. Worse, what if someone wants to schedule a play date?

It's a huge surprise, then, during Jake's preschool orientation, when I hear myself agree to the role of "Room Mommy," the person who organizes the classroom holiday parties. "I'll do it," I blurt, when the teacher requests a volunteer.

Chris looks at me sideways, eyebrows raised.

I elbow him and stare straight ahead.

"Delightful!" Linda says. She's standing in front of a flip-chart that has the alphabet printed on it in bright primary colors.

With a flick of her gray-flecked bob, she hands me an envelope containing $60 cash and a hand-written note that says: Halloween, Winter, Valentine's Day. Bring drinks, snacks, treat bags and crafts for 16 kids. Thanks!

In the car, I say, "Crap," as I finger the bills. Secretly, I think about heading right to the liquor store to buy a few bottles of wine.

"You're not really a room mom type," says Chris.

I roll my eyes. "Thanks."

"Why on earth did you volunteer?"

I shrug. "I don't know."

But I did know. It was because of Facebook. I couldn't say this out loud, because Chris dislikes Facebook as much as I detest the word "kiddos." It's not that I *enjoy* social media, but it compels me sometimes. If I turn on my computer and don't have a set destination, I often find myself wandering over to Facebook, my fingers automatically typing my username and password. As I scroll through the status updates, it reminds me of looking into people's windows when I'm walking down a street in a new country, trying to see what people are doing in the kitchen, living room, or even the bedroom.

A couple days prior, I'd found myself on Facebook, inadvertently caught in the crossfire of a Mommy War battle. The post that pulled the trigger (*parents, start your engines*) was written by a woman whose profile photo I didn't recognize, yet is apparently my "friend." It said:

OMG! Lily is reading! She's only 3. Guess her preschool is doing something right.

My shoulders tensed and my right heel started thumping the floor. It was a clear cue for me to stop, to look the other way, but I didn't. I sat there, glued to the screen, reading all thirty-seven comments, in which people discussed the local preschool scene. One mom boasted that her two-year-old son was already identifying numbers and letters, which she credited to her kid's "academic preschool." Another said she supported Montessori education and assured everyone that this was the best approach for the "whole child." Dozens of women chimed in, "liking" their favorite comments in the thread, adding logos to various racecars, insisting that their school was the best. There were representatives from a mind-numbing variety of categories, considering the kids they were talking about are (roughly) four-year-olds, and the local public school system ranks academically well in the state and nation. There was Waldorf, Methodist, Catholic, cooperative, academic, bi-lingual, global, Montessori, plus two public school supporters. Some preschools offered optional gymnastics, lunch bunch, or special music programs. Moms with children younger than Elise had already researched schools, made a list of their Top 3, put their kids on waiting lists, and told their husbands to "get a second job," since it seemed that sometimes tuition costs as much as a mortgage.

I was stunned. I'd simply enrolled Jake in the public preschool that was a half mile from our house. It was inside a classroom in his to-be elementary school, and I thought that was quaint. I'd been excited that we could walk there, following the river the whole time. We could hold hands, squeezing back and forth, enjoying nature and talking.

Clearly, I'd failed. I wanted to boast camaraderie with these mothers on Facebook, saying something in the comments like,

"Wow, that is so awesome that Franny can read *Spot Goes to School* before she's potty trained! My kid can…"

But I had nothing to report. Jake liked dancing to hip hop music? And he often beat me at the game Memory? There were, of course, his toy cars and motorcycles and boats, which he invented new scenarios for each day. And the guns he was making out of everything, including his granola bars. (Certainly I couldn't share that. They'd force me to enroll him in the one preschool that had a mental health team.) I read him books every day but hadn't thought of focusing on anything academic. I was taking him out into the world and introducing him to experiences. Wasn't this enough?

Apparently not. I clicked off Facebook, fearing my child would be "left behind," just like the controversial legislation, and it would be my fault. So when the opportunity to volunteer in Jake's classroom presented itself, it felt almost serendipitous. Certainly this type of thing is what good mommies did. Maybe I'd failed when I hadn't spent hours researching his school, but I could make up for lost time. I could prove that I, too, was dedicated to my child's future.

———

In the car driving away from the preschool, Chris begins The List–all the reasons it's not a good idea for me to take this Room Mommy volunteer position. *I'm too busy. I don't like crafts. I barely decorate our house for holidays. When we have parties, I just send people to the fridge for their own drinks.* His points are all valid, but it's this same annoying dynamic again; me expressing a new idea, and him immediately responding with a negative attitude.

"Stop it," I say. "You're doing it again."

He frowns. "What am I *doing* again?"

"Being all negative when I bring up an idea."

"Fine. I won't talk."

"Whatever." I shift my mind back to this task I've agreed to. I mean, what do you even put in a treat bag? The last time I did a holiday art project I was around seven years old. My mind immediately fills with images of kitschy crafts—stuffed felt pumpkins and stocking Santas and lollypop Valentines. *Ugh.*

But I will not give up. I will prove to Chris that I am a great Room Mommy. I will show Jake that I'm interested in his first school experience. I will do this and then post the status on Facebook. "Threw the best Room Mommy party ever and my son's whole class loves me!" Maybe, if I'm clever, I can even find a statistic on how this will positively affect Jake's educational future.

Over the next weeks, I feel paralyzed. I think a half dozen times about calling Linda to tell her I made a mistake, but then time gets away, like it does, and before I know it, I've procrastinated long enough that it's almost Halloween, and I can't do that to Linda, who is undoubtedly trying to help my son catch up academically to all of his classmates. On a foggy morning in late October, I sit down to make my own list.

Pushing my hair behind my ear, I write: candy, stickers. Orange juice? Then my mind goes blank. I set down my pen and chew on my barely there thumb nail. What's orange and black and edible and interesting for four-year-olds? Probably I should join Pinterest to get some ideas; thousands of mommies must have boards full of kid-tastic party tips.

Nah. Nothing about Pinterest interests me.

What are my options? I could buy a tray of frosted cookies, but that seems boring. And actually, I should probably add something that would enhance a core subject in some way–reading, math, or science. Like maybe an experiment with dry ice and a cauldron! Or a witch word search. But wait, Jake can't read, and if all his classmates can read, then he'll feel stupid. And then he'll hate me. And then he'll never squeeze my hand again.

I abandon the list. Too much pressure.

"Jake and Elise," I yell. "Let's go for a walk by the river."

They come scampering. I throw a few things into the stroller—snacks, water, diapers—while they haphazardly pull on their shoes. My friends marvel at my apparent ability to just get up and go with two kids, but I wouldn't describe it as easy. It's slow and laborious and mind-boggling, just like negotiating prices in *pesos* at an outdoor market in Oaxaca, converting each counter-offer into dollars, or trying to deal with the *Arbeitsamt* in Germany. The act of leaving the house takes a lot of effort, no less than twenty minutes, involving Jake tying his shoes, Elise trying to find her shoes, Jake feeling frustrated with tying his shoes, Elise deciding she wants to wear a different pair of shoes, Jake crying, Elise whining, me just pulling them out the door, thinking, *Fuck it, if we forgot something we're only a few minutes from home.* From the outside, it looks seamless.

As we wander the path, I embrace the joy on my kids' faces as they pick up sticks, toss rocks into the water, and look for ducks. Jake's blue eyes shine. Elise's feet patter the ground. We stand on the pedestrian bridge overhanging the river, sticking our noses through the metal bars, searching for fish in the water. I think back to before I had kids, when I'd occasionally envision myself as a mother with a toddler throwing stones in the river. In many ways, the reality is shockingly similar. I teach them words: mallard, boulder, current—and watch them integrate the meaning into their surroundings. I love mothering in environments like this, where life is stripped down.

That's what I valued before having kids, and nothing has changed. But so many women seem to magically transform the minute the umbilical cord is cut, going from "regular adult" to "Mommy," gaining a whole new vocabulary. They are especially vocal on Facebook, posting dozens of updates about their children and using abbreviations like "DD" to mean darling daughter, or "HTH" for Hope This Helps—foreign codes—as well as sharing their strong opinions about everything from time outs to spanking to daycare. They go from talking about politics and driving a sedan pre-motherhood, to purchasing a bus-sized vehicle and replacing their Facebook profile photo with one of their baby. People seem to think this is an excellent way to scream, "I am a great mom!" But I think it's a subtle way of surrendering one's core identity. A mother is not her baby. I want to write snarky comments on the photos like, "Oh my God, what happened? You turned into an infant! Gross!"

I know. This makes me The Snobbiest Mommy on the Block. But really, it's just loneliness seeping in again. Motherhood feels like adolescence all over again, when every other girl got breasts before me, and I sat in the corner wondering if I would ever be like them. The problem is, I'm thirty-eight years old now, which means I'm not likely to grow into anything I'm not already. It's hard to accept that I'm never going to measure up.

———

In the candy aisle of the grocery store, I scour the shelves for Halloween treats that seem creative. Jake bounces around, picking up every crinkly bag he can find. Elise sits in the cart, mesmerized.

I hold up smiling jack-o-lantern stickers. "Jake, do you like these?" I ask.

Jake glances over. "Yeah!"

"What about these?" It's a box of ghost tattoos.

"Cool!"

I throw both items into the cart, as well as some orange cellophane bags. Jake seems satisfied with these simple items, so I head to the produce section to explore orange and black fruits and veggies. A woman with a toddler and an overflowing cart passes by. She's collected plastic pumpkins, floppy witches, orange crazy straws, glow sticks, huge bags of candy—a cornucopia of Halloween spirit. A real-life Pinterest board. I bet she's planning her kid's party, too. I freeze. *Is this what I'm supposed to do?* For a second, I think about rolling an apple under the wheel of her cart to distract her, and then stealing what's inside.

"Hi," she says, ignoring me and looking at Elise. "You are so cute! How old are you? Seventeen months? Eighteen?"

"She's two."

The woman looks at me. "Oh gosh, she's tiny!"

Thanks for the reminder, I think. But I say, "Oh, well. She's petite."

She shrugs. "Isn't this fun! All this Halloween stuff."

I look at her cart. "Uh huh."

"Well, I'm having a bunch of kids at my house." She taps her child on the head and says to him, "Aren't we, Finn? Aren't we having a party?"

He nods.

"Cool," I say. I really mean it.

She looks at her son again. "We mommies sure do love this!" she announces. And I think: *Some mommies love this.*

Then she looks up at me. "Hey, did you see those life-size skeletons over there. You have to buy one of those!! And, oh my God, the glitter witches!"

I shift on my feet uncomfortably and turn my cart slightly in the other direction. As she talks, I discreetly walk away, leaving her alone with her festive obsessions. In the next aisle, I consider going back for the glitter witches—the kids probably would like that. But then I think, *No.* More than I want to fit in to this foreign world of mommy-madness, I want to model my authentic self for my children. I stride over to the produce section and scan the bins for orange and black veggies and fruits. I choose Clementine oranges and black grapes and hope for the best.

On the morning of the party, I put on a nice pair of jeans and a tunic and pouf on some blush. As I place the party items in a box, I realize it looks like a paltry offering. My stomach drops. I wish I could disappear. I think about running to the store to grab a few more things—maybe the glitter witches are still there, and oh shit, I forgot all about incorporating an academic activity—but it's too late. I check my email, and then find myself (I can't help it) on Facebook.

But before I even read the first post on my wall, I change my mind. I opt out. I turn away from the window. "Willpower," I say. This is not the time to make myself feel negative and inferior and judgmental, which is what Facebook does 98% of the time. Instead, I visit one of my favorite outdoor mom blogs and read a quick post about how she took her kids stand-up paddleboarding on a reservoir near her house. This blogger is a woman I've never met, but her posts always inspire me, and I'd love to meet her someday. She's part of my tribe. I make a mental note to try SUPing as a family next summer. I smile, realizing how much better my time was spent, reading something positive, connecting with my tribe, instead of getting caught up in things that make me feel less than fulfilled.

Because the truth is, I don't care if my kids can read before every other kid. I want them to be healthy and happy and loved, and they are.

At the party, the kids are decked out in their princess and superhero costumes, laughing and playing and dancing. Jake shows me around his classroom, pointing to an easel where he paints, and to a desk where he practices his handwriting. There's also a Red Square for kids who need a time-out, but Jake assures me he's never been in there. During "free choice," he says he usually chooses to play in the toy kitchen or at the art station.

The kids do a class performance to the song "Monster Mash," beaming as all the parents beam back. I bite my bottom lip. Jake looks so proud as he stares right at me, sharing his first school experience with me. And I am proud to be his Room Mommy.

After the dance, it's snack time. The kids barely notice the specifics of the treat. I watch Jake in his firefighter costume, hanging out with his friends, chatting incessantly as he peels his orange. He tells every one of his friends that *his* Mommy planned the party. I smile.

Toward the end of the event, Linda calls me to the front of the room. She pats me on the back. "Thank you to Jake's mom for planning this!" she announces.

Everyone claps. I stand there, blushing, as she gushes about the wonderful job I've done. I'm pretty sure she tells this to every Room Mommy. But then later she pulls me aside and says, "This really is the best party. Wonderfully simple," she whispers.

Inside, I glow. This accomplishment ranks up with other difficult things I've done in my life, because I jumped out of my comfort zone and stuck to my values. Admittedly, the snarky part of me wants to stand on a chair screaming, "Take that, Mommies!" And then write a bragging Facebook post and text Chris a list of why it *was* a good idea for me to do this volunteer project. But I don't. Because above all, I want to enjoy the rest of the party. And then I want to walk home along the river with my son.

14

Sidecar Sally

Four and a Half Years into Motherhood

It's first light on my second day in Yelapa, Mexico, and I'm in a panga boat skimming the peaked ripples of the Banderas Bay. A dozen huddled passengers surround me on wooden benches—local Mexicans of all ages, smiling and chatting, traveling to Puerto Vallarta for the day.

"Amigo!" one guy yells to another, over the roar of the motor. He slaps him on the back.

I squint into the wind and chew on my thumbnail, jittery with excitement. I'm not going to Puerto Vallarta. At a tiny beach, a stop on the way to the city, I'm jumping out of the boat and meeting two or three strange men.

Tom, my landlord, called my *casita* yesterday. "We're touring the jungle backroads tomorrow," he said. "Join us?"

I paused. I thought he was calling to make sure I had hot water and a cold refrigerator. "I thought there were really no roads," I said.

"There aren't."

"Uh huh."

"We can probably make it, with the Jeep."

"Who's going?"

"Not sure. Possibly an American photographer and a crazy Australian dude who's been traveling for eight years."

I took a long, slow sip of my Pacifico. During this week away from Chris and the kids, I'd planned to be anti-social: to write and walk and sleep. No agenda. I'd found Yelapa on the Internet, and I had an intuitively good feeling about it, because the only map of the region was hand drawn. I was looking forward to lacing up my boots and exploring.

This was my first big solo trip since Elise's birth a year and a half ago, partly because I simply hadn't wanted to leave. The scare with her health made me pull her in tight, and I was hesitant to let her go–ever. The most I'd done was a few overnights. Twice, I'd come back early, unable to relax without her near me.

The other reason was childcare. If arranging babysitting during my travels with one child was like a 500-piece puzzle, with two kids, it was more like 1,500 pieces. I could hear that nagging echo–*"one plus one equals three!"* Jake needed to be dropped off and picked up from preschool, but Elise wasn't in daycare and still took naps. As competent as Chris was, it was a lot to manage alone. My leaving felt like a burden.

But when I discovered Yelapa and Chris saw that look in my eyes, we worked out this trip. I was beginning to feel really good in my body and mind again, just like I'd remembered feeling when Jake was about a year and a half old, when I rode around on my Harley.

So, on the phone with Tom, tempted with the possibility of a rugged adventure, I decided I had to go. I couldn't pass it up. When was the last time I did something this spontaneous?

"In," I said.

"Great. Meet us at Boca. Wear your bikini."

In the boat, I reach behind my neck and tighten the straps of my swimsuit under my dress. I brought two bikinis on this trip, and I'm wearing the one that's far more conservative—neutral tones, full coverage, visually boring. I know from Tom's website that in addition to renting *casas* in the village of Yelapa, he's a bikini photographer.

Obviously, I'm not a bikini model. I'm winter white, I recently cut my hair short, and of course, I've birthed two children in the last four years. I love wearing bikinis—soft strings grazing skin—but the thought of being captured on film while frolicking in a jungle waterfall makes me feel self-conscious, some unflattering pose trapped forever and posted who-knows-where. If Tom photographs me, I'm hoping my suit will blend into the earth, making me invisible.

I gaze out at the waves and search for the humpback whales that give birth in these warm waters each winter. There's only a jagged, hazy cliff in the distance. It feels symbolic. I am a mother, bypassing typical tourist destinations for a trip into wild places with strange men, in a country that's notorious for its warring drug cartels. My father would say, "Didn't I teach you better?" He'd ask me to remember the time I got stuck in Wyoming with a flat tire. "Do you want that to happen again?" he'd ask.

Water splashes up around the boat and grazes my eye. It feels like a tear. I wipe it away.

At the beach, Tom waves. He looks harmless enough: early forties, sandals, genuine smile. "Morning, Carrie," he says.

I babble. "Hi. I almost missed the boat. I couldn't hear my alarm clock over the sound of the waves. My neighbor knocked on my door. Ha!" I glance back toward the boat. It's gone.

He laughs. "Glad you made it." He adjusts the strap of his camera bag and leads me up a cobblestone path through a maze of haphazardly parked cars. I scan Tom for anything that seems sketchy: knives, drugs, guns. Nothing. My instinct says he's trustworthy, but sometimes it's tricky to tell.

I buy a Coke Light from an open-air *tienda*. A beautiful black-eyed boy, about Jake's age, stares at me from behind the counter. "*Buenos dias*," I say, sweetly. He buries his face in his mother's skirt. Guilt stabs my belly. Jake is getting dressed for preschool right now. Elise is probably wandering around the house saying, "Mama?"

Last night, I sent Chris an email that said, "I'm touring the jungle tomorrow with Tom, my landlord. If you don't hear from me within 24 hours, send out a search party. XO."

Ten minutes later, he replied, "Have fun! Love you." But I could see his concern, even through the make-believe jungle of Cyberspace. I knew I should share his feelings.

As I exit the *tienda*, I see Tom talking to two white guys. They're near a well-worn Toyota 4-Runner and a badass motorcycle with a sidecar—flat black with a pile of spare tires, and a helmet strapped to the back rack.

The guy with the cigarette reaches his hand out to shake mine. "Hi," he says. "I'm Joe." Three words and I know he's the

Aussie. I take in his wild black hair and boots and faded jeans. *Crazy, maybe.* But he averts his eyes when he looks at me, which seems sweet and shy, respectful. He reminds me of a famous poster of James Dean.

The other guy is an ebullient American. "I'm Brian," he says. He has short clipped brown hair and a point-and-shoot camera in his hand, yet he must be the photographer. He says he's a vagabond.

Tom gives me a mischievous smile. "We've decided you're going to ride in the sidecar. We voted before you got here."

It feels like a test. *What else did they discuss before I arrived?*

"Great," I say, feigning confidence. "I love motorcycles. I had a Harley."

They all look surprised. When I look down, I can see why. I look nothing like a biker chick. I'm dressed like I didn't know what to expect today, like maybe I'm going to the beach, or on a hike: brown sundress, flip flops, black fleece. I'm carrying a blue mesh bag that contains a towel, water, protein bars, and camera.

Joe looks at my painted blue toenails and half-smiles. "Do you have boots?" he asks.

"No. But I have running shoes." Really, they're little sneakers.

He snuffs out his cigarette with his toe. "Good. Because you might need to push, if the roads are bad."

———

I love riding in the sidecar. The air is brisk, blowing my hair into wild tangles. I pull the leather seat cover up to my chest, snuggle back into the cushion and watch the palm trees of the jungle canopy morph into pines and shrubs as we climb. Not unlike the landscape of Colorado. As I peer through the trees, I look for dead bodies or surly drug lords wielding machetes or machine guns. It's wild out there, but no blood.

Joe navigates the curves of the road. There's an instant ease between us that strikes me. He hands me his hat. I hold it. I point to an interesting sign. He nods. We don't talk, and we know almost nothing about each other, but it feels like we've been traveling together for months. I sense something awakening in me—what is it? I can't put my finger on it, but it feels important.

When we stop for a rest, I don't want to. Except that we're in the driveway of a breathtaking botanical garden, a display of color and texture and sound. There are hot pink bouganvillas, manicured fruit trees, frolicking dogs, a beautiful open-air restaurant containing wooden tables and benches. Birds chirp. Dishes clank in a nearby kitchen. The air smells like sunshine.

Brian saunters over. "How was the sidecar?"

"Awesome."

"You weren't cold?"

"Not really."

Tom kneels down. He snaps a photo of me stepping out of the sidecar. I giggle. He keeps shooting. I wave my hand in the air. "Take some photos of Joe," I say.

We tour the botanical gardens, which has dozens of varieties of orchids, water lilies, and tropical plants. Tom knows interesting details about the flora, like that vanilla is part of the orchid family. I snap a few photos, so I will remember.

As I climb back into the sidecar, Joe says, "You like it in there, huh?"

I smile. "I do."

He gives me a long, amused look.

Brian pipes in. "I guess we should call you Sidecar Sally."

Everyone laughs. It's not until we're rumbling out of the driveway that I realize Brian is right on. It's Sidecar Sally awakening inside of me, the part of my identity that exists opposite my role as wife and mother. She's fearless and free-spirited, the woman who takes road trips through Wyoming and Montana, or backpacks alone into the mountains with barely a plan, or camps in the desert to deal with fear about the results of her daughter's newborn screen. I'd never given her a name.

We order margaritas at a hacienda in the middle of nowhere. I choose passion fruit with *raicilla,* the local moonshine. The place is a palace, with high ceilings, dark mahogany woodwork and windows overlooking hillsides of trees and vines. Even the women's bathroom is beautiful, with ornate sinks and elegant artwork.

We wander around individually, checking things out. Joe and I end up at the same window.

"How long are you in Yelapa, Sidecar Sally?" he asks.

I smile. "A while."

"And then where are you going?"

I pause. "Home?"

Joe laughs.

I give him a brotherly push. "Where are you going next?"

"Next? Copper Canyon."

I've heard of this region in Chihuahua. Some of the canyons are as deep as the Grand.

"Have you been there?" he asks.

I shake my head. "No."

Joe tells me he's traveling from Argentina to Alaska by motorcycle, and before that he bicycled across Africa.

"Wow," I say, rapt. I can imagine myself doing all of those things.

He lifts his camera and takes a photo.

"So, do you like traveling solo?" I ask. I expect him to say *hell yeah, I love it.*

"Not really," he says. "I'd like to share this experience with someone." He pauses. "But it would have to be the right woman."

My breath catches. I lean down to scratch my leg and create a subtle change in subject. I gasp. There are pinpricks of blood covering my calves, ankles, and feet. Tiny wings flutter. I spring up. "My legs!" I exclaim.

Tom looks over from the table. "Carrie! Those are No-see-um bites," he says. "Quick. Get some bug spray."

I run over to a table at the edge of the patio where I saw a tube of white cream. I slather it over my legs. But the damage is already done. Swollen welts cover my calves, ankles, and feet. I didn't even know it was happening. From the knees down, I look like I've been living in a cave in the jungle for months, like I am physically morphing into my alter ego.

The wife and mother in me would've put on insect repellent as a preventive measure. But Sidecar Sally doesn't give a shit. What's a few bug bites?

When the road becomes dirt, we go fast. It's fun and dusty and carefree, and we skid around in the sand, but I'm not scared. I can't stop smiling. In a way, this feels like a glimpse into a life I might've chosen, one without marriage and children. I'm happy with my choices—I wouldn't change them. And I think I could have been happy this way, too. World travel punctuated by longer stays in special places, a string of lovers, or sidecars, or endless dance partners.

I know there would be disadvantages: feelings of loneliness and displacement. Joe admits he wants companionship. But as much as I try to be content inside my white picket fence in Colorado, changing diapers and cooking macaroni and cheese, Sidecar Sally whispers—and sometimes screams—her need for freedom. Domesticity versus wanderlust. It's an ongoing match.

When we reach the waterfall, I spring out of the sidecar. I trudge through the river ahead of the guys, toss my flip-flops onto the shore, and peel off my dress on a pale boulder. Tom's carrying his camera bag, but I don't even care. I don't care that my body isn't perfect, or that I'm in the jungle with three men, or that I'm not a typical mother. I hope we get stuck and that I have to push the motorcycle. I hope we're forced to park the bike above Yelapa so we can hike down at dusk into the village.

I wade into the thigh-deep cold water and stoop down to submerge my whole body. The tender skin on my chest, covering my heart, prickles. "Ooh," I say. "Yes." I walk on my hands through the pool, the sand rough under my palms, kicking my legs behind me.

Under the rush of the waterfall, I stand up. Water pummels my back and my head and my neck. It feels like a fist, or a passionate heartbeat. I squeeze my eyes shut. I breathe hard. Everything else disappears.

When I step out of the cascade and rub open my eyes, they're all there. Tom is kneeling on a rock, snapping photos of me. Joe and Brian stand on the edge of the pool in their swim trunks. They look so innocent.

"Am I the only one who's swimming?" I tease.

They stare at me like I'm crazy.

"Isn't it cold?" says Brian.

"Yeah," says Joe.

I shrug. "It's great!"

Tom looks up from his camera. His whole face lights up. "Sidecar Sally," he says, "I've never seen anyone enjoy a waterfall like that."

I throw my hands in the air. "Thank you."

———

We stumble upon a ranch owned by Tom's friends. The landscape is dust and brush and scattered trees. A lone azalea catches my eye, and I take in the burst of color. I feel like that right now: a bright bloom. I brush my hair from my face and do a little salsa step in the dirt.

"This town has forty people," Tom says.

I look around at the smattering of small structures. "Town?"

"Yep."

"Whoa."

We wander up onto the sweeping ranch porch. An elderly

Mexican man with leathery skin hugs Tom and pours us each a shot of *raicilla.*

"Cheers!" I exclaim, clinking each glass. I shoot mine; they sip.

Tom leads us to an adjacent house with a dirt floor, where a teenaged girl is making tortillas. The air smells like smoke and earth. The girl looks up shyly when she sees all of us staring.

"*Hola,*" I say, trying to make eye contact. She blushes.

I watch as she mixes cornmeal with water and places a ball of dough into a ceramic hand press. She pulls down the handle—*thump*—and nods, satisfied. With a graceful flick of her wrist, she tosses the tortilla onto a skillet over a wood stove. It sizzles. I am amazed by so many things: her ability to keep the fire at the right temperature, the perfection of her circles, the fact that she makes tortillas twice every day.

"*Bueno,*" I say, clapping my hands.

The guys goad me, so I agree to give it a try. It's way harder than it looks. I fumble around with the dough, which sticks to my fingers, creating a gooey mess in my palms. Every one of my tortillas is torn or misshapen or stuck to the press. I laugh, but it comes out sounding more uncomfortable than carefree. I look at the girl, and then the men, and something shifts deep in my gut. I have an urge to tell them: *I am a good cook. I make delicious lasagna. I take my kids to the playground and read them books.*

Instead, I wipe my hands on a towel and walk away. I wander past the painted white church, scattered wooden houses, free-range cattle. Children dart past. I smile and wave.

At the one-room schoolhouse, I stop and peer in the windows. Joe appears behind me.

"Check out those desks," I say. "They're wooden, like old times."

He laughs and points to the wall, which is covered in hand-painted pictures. I wonder if Jake is painting a picture right now at his school, or practicing his letters.

Joe turns to face me. "Hey Carrie?" he asks.

"Yeah?"

"I was wondering. Do you want to see Copper Canyon?"

In my head, Sidecar Sally screams, *Yes! You do! This is a once-in-a-lifetime opportunity!*

"Do you?" asks Joe.

I scratch my leg, and then look back at the children's pictures. "I would love to," I say. "But I can't."

He seems unfazed. "Okay."

I smile and try to act normal. But inside I feel raw, like fingernails are scratching my flesh. I look back toward the house where the girl is making tortillas. I imagine her holding up a ball of dough the shape of Sidecar Sally's heart. She places it on the press. The handle descends and smashes it flat. On the fire, it burns.

———

Two days later, I'm still reeling over my decision, so I schedule a massage with a therapist in Yelapa. Maybe her hands can purge my body of longing and knead some sense into me. I walk the path to the therapy room and it's nothing fancy—a large pop-up nylon tent with a massage table inside, blending, as does everything in Yelapa, with the natural world. I undress completely. As I lie naked under a thin sheet, staring at the dirt ground, waiting for my massage to begin, I try to relax, to let my mind release any thoughts.

The therapist enters, and without saying a word, turns the sheet down to my waist and begins to slide her hands down my shoulders and spine. I melt into the table. "So," she says, making light conversation. "What have you been doing in Yelapa?" Instead of admitting I need silence during my massage in order to find a meditative place, I find myself telling her about my life in Colorado, and then recounting, in great detail, my foray into the jungle with Tom and Joe and Brian.

"Wow," she says. "Your voice lights up when you talk about that."

I swallow. My throat tightens.

"Sounds like you really needed that. That break. That freedom."

At this, I begin crying. And then sobbing. Tears roll off my face and soak the sheets, and even drip to the ground, making little dents in the sand. My nose runs and I sniffle and I'm a complete slobbering mess and embarrassed at my reaction, yet I can't make myself stop.

Since I can't stop, she does. The therapist places her hands, side by side, in the middle of my back and just stands there, letting her heat meet mine. She doesn't speak. The touch feels good, and the warmth of her hands soaks deep into my body, into my core, and comforts me. The feeling reminds me of when Chris and I sleep belly to back, curled together, one. And somehow, as she stands there, silent, it feels like her hands are gluing my heart back together. Putting *me* back together. I feel myself becoming whole. It affirms how much I needed to honor

Sidecar Sally, who is an important part of my identity, and to give her a name. I needed to let her live and breathe and flourish.

And now she needs to meld with my center. She must co-exist with the other parts of who I am: she is not the whole me. I am equal parts wife, mother, Sidecar Sally, and more. I brush the tears from my eyes, exhale, and re-focus. The therapist begins to move her hands. We move onward.

15

Tough Love

Four Years, Eight Months into Motherhood

It is mid-morning on day three of a trek through Arizona's Paria Canyon, and two of my toes are numb. The trail crosses the river again and again, with no bridges, and each time I step into the icy water, my feet recoil with needle-like pain. I look down at my mesh shoes and imagine the skin underneath, wrinkled and white, purple veins pulsing life. "Damn," I say, searching for a patch of sunlight. Yesterday I discovered that even a thin golden ray can provide comfort that feels like a pair of wool socks.

But no light reaches the canyon floor just yet. I scrutinize a sunny spot high up on the rock wall. *Forty-five minutes*, I estimate, *before the warmth creeps all the way down.*

Downstream, my friends Adam and Seth are two curves ahead, because I said I needed space. It's an odd request out here where everything echoes, but I'm on vacation from mothering, exhausted from being touched and asked questions and needed. When Adam announced at a party that he was planning this trip with some guy friends, I said, "Take me!" We didn't know each other well, but he shrugged and said, "Sure."

Chris said, "Go for it."

Adam looked at Chris. "Really?"

"Fine with me. I'm going on a guy's camping trip later this summer. This will be her 'guys' trip."

We laughed.

Adam's wife was also all for it. She didn't have any desire to walk a canyon for several days and said something like, "If he can find someone else to do this stuff with, then I don't have to."

But this wasn't really about co-ed camping trips; it was about taking turns. It made me think of something a friend said. Just like Chris and me, she and her husband tag team their adventures. They love skiing and paddling rivers, and even with two kids, they still manage to keep going, with a simple understanding. She skis on Saturday; him on Sunday. She runs the first section on the river; him the second. They shuttle for each other, watch for each other, take turns at home with the baby, and then always meet back up for post-adventure celebrations.

Chris and I do the same thing. When he goes jogging or runs races, I'm on kid duty. When I go to yoga, he's on duty. Sometimes this looks a lot like passing a baton in a relay. He'll come in the door from a jog, and I'll hand him the diaper bag and dash out to a class. In the evenings after the kids are in bed, we share wine or beer at the dinner table, recounting our experiences. It's a true team effort.

And now, here I am on my "guy's trip" while Chris is at home on duty for a few days. As for Adam and Seth and me, we're comrades in a canyon: together, apart, united in our mission.

At the edge of the river, I bend down to massage my toes. With hypothermia, is it tingling that's a warning? Extended numbness? Pain? Using my thumbs and forefingers, I wiggle each toe individually, urging blood through my veins, willing myself forward. Although we don't have a route map for this trek (the park office was closed), Adam estimates that our hike today is ten miles, which will take us to our car. *I can make it.* I stand up and jog in place for a few seconds, my pack thumping around on my back. My left ankle wobbles. My right knee almost buckles.

"Okay," I say, glaring at the river. With a giant inhale, I dip my right foot into the calf-deep water and tramp to the other side.

It's easy to fall into a rhythm—plod, splash, plod, splash—and I tousle my wispy hair and survey my surroundings: a weaving of water and land, wholly unlike my familiar Colorado mountain terrain. The contrasts are stark: Red rock piercing blue sky. Milky water lapping mud. Pale grasses nudging pine. I look over my shoulder at my footprints, tiny divots in vast sand.

I wanted to feel physically strong on this trip, but I don't. My calves are thick knots, my left ankle is swelling, and both shoulders zing with pain. Despite all my efforts—yoga and cycling and hiking—my body feels sloppy after two rounds of childbirth; abdominal muscles stretchy and soft.

But I'm here, right? And I'm doing this? Deep inside, my core burns bright. I imagine the burger and salad I'll eat later in celebration.

Up ahead, I see my companions talking to a group of hikers with a map–the first people we've seen in a day. I amble up. "Hey."

Adam runs a hand through his copper hair. "Hi."

"What's up?"

Everyone looks at me uncomfortably.

Finally, Adam speaks. "It turns out we might've been wrong on our distance."

"Oh." I nod like it's no big deal. *How bad can it be?*

"We have around twenty more miles."

My jaw drops. "What?"

"Yeah."

"Twenty. From here?" I hear my voice rising. The entire trail is thirty-eight miles. How do we still have more than half of those to hike?

"Holy shit," I whisper. I stride to a dry spot, throw off my backpack, and lean forward, hands on my knees. The sun is arcing up overhead, and suddenly I feel hot and thirsty. I look over at Seth, hoping he'll laugh and say this is a joke. But he's silent, staring down at his drenched boots, his lanky frame slumped.

In my head, I fume. *How did this happen? Why didn't we insist on a map? Why did I trust these guys? This sucks. I can't hike twenty more miles.*

I look up. "We have to camp one more night."

Seth shrugs. "But our permit ends today."

"So what. I'll talk to the rangers, beg for forgiveness."

We stand there in silence. The other hikers move on. Overhead, a bird screams.

Adam places a hand in the pocket of his khaki pants. He sighs and urges me on with a nod. "Let's just keep hiking and see what happens."

I can tell by the look in his eyes that he has no intention of camping. He's an enthusiastic type, and today that means he's ready to rock out these last miles, hit the trail hard, even if it requires strapping on our head lamps at dusk and hiking into the night.

I bite my bottom lip, holding back a torrent of angry words. I fasten my pack. "Fine. But I am not crossing the river in the dark."

Adam and Seth have already begun walking.

I follow step, furious, clomping around in the sand. *Fucking trail. Fucking canyon. Fucking us, who spent more than two days using the sun to gauge our time and distance. Only idiots do that. Amateurs.*

Within ten minutes, I am so far behind I can't see my comrades. My promise to "pick up the pace" was half-hearted, because I can't seem to make my legs go any faster, and also I don't want to. Every day as a mother of two children involves running from one place to the next, preparing bags full of supplies, and making the most of every free second. On vacation, I want to go slow. *If I have to*, I think, *I will camp solo tonight.* Everything's on my back: one-person tent, sleeping bag, energy bars. My family's not expecting me back for a few days. No one will worry.

But then I look down at my feet. My left ankle has ballooned out to the same width as my calf. If I take my shoe off to sleep, I won't get it back on in the morning. *Will I even be able to walk in the morning?*

I stomp my right foot in the dust. "Shit!" I scream. It echoes four times, which isn't enough. *Shit*, I whisper. *Shit.*

I stumble forward, grasping the straps of my pack. My heart thumps against my knuckles. I think of the hardest things I've done in my life: Olympic-distance triathlons. Dancing on raw, bleeding toes in a ballet company throughout adolescence. Climbing up rocks and mountains. But nothing seems harder than this, than what lies ahead.

I walk fast and breathe fast and listen to the sound of my backpack squeaking against my lower back. Something about this sensation—the rhythm—brings a new word to mind. Childbirth. *The hardest thing I've ever done, hands down.*

The C-section was one thing, but Elise's home birth was grueling. That entire night of teeth-gnashing, bone-shaking, flesh-ripping pain. I remember insisting on going in the bathtub, and then hating the bathtub. Begging for drugs. Flailing and wailing. And the midwife responding with tough love. "You wanted this," she said. It was the most un-magical experience of my life, yet I made it, and it produced the most dazzling ending: Elise.

And for this reason alone, ironic but true, I know I will finish this hike. Motherhood is *why* I can do this. My steel mind will urge my weak body to simply keep walking.

I press my damp hair behind my ear, groan at the cramping in my lower back, and forge forward. It is miles of sand, boulders, and jagged rock crevices, always threading the river. Each step sends waves of pain through my body, and I focus on the forward motion of my hips, imagining them strong and flexible–up to the task. Slowly, quietly, while humming a tune I remember from yoga, I retreat to a deep primal place. It's that spot I remember from childbirth, as old as the earth, where my resolve exists naked and pure. The place Chris described as trance-like, faraway. But I'm not far away, really; I'm painstakingly close—operating from the deep wild of my core.

In this place, time stops. Hours pass. Daylight fades. The beam of a headlamp guides my way. Stars glitter overhead, sand swooshes underfoot, thickets scratch against my pants.

When I finally emerge into my conscious mind, it's to the yelps and broad smiles of my companions. "Look over there," says Adam. "Do you see that?" I squint into the black night. Barely, I can make out the dark hump of our car.

"Yes!" I scream, triumphant. Fully alive, I start walking, and then run-walking, and then running, unfastening the straps of my pack. "We made it!"

I collapse into the front seat of the car, a lump of human flesh, my headlamp still beaming. But my smile outshines the light. Somehow, some way, this is just what I wanted.

16

Sweet Summit

Five Years into Motherhood

There is a ghost-like presence in the doorway of the bedroom. I can feel it in my bones in the pitch dark, even though I'm half asleep. My eyes pop open and my heart skips a beat and I hold my breath. "What the?" I whisper. The clock says 6:20 a.m. My mind races. I think *intruder? Wayward neighbor? Animal?* Automatically, my hand reaches toward the edge of the bed, because the baseball bat is hidden underneath.

But then the form speaks. "Mommy?" I look closer and realize it's five-year-old Jake. I exhale. He does this sometimes; shows up in our doorway and stands there, and it startles me anew every time.

"Darling," I say, "What are you doing? Is something wrong?"

"Hi Mommy!" he exclaims brightly.

Squinting in the dim light through my drooping eyes, I see that Jake is fully dressed, wearing his hiking clothes: dry-fit shirt, zip-off pants, ball cap. "The sun's up," he announces, pointing to a thin ray of gray light slipping in through a slat in our blinds.

"Okay, honey," I say. "We'll get up soon."

"But I want to go camping. You said we would go when the sun comes up. Did you pack a flashlight? Should I wake Elise up? I want waffles for breakfast."

"Oh, buddy," I say, laughing and throwing my arms over my face. The kid is all *go*; he wakes up at dawn every day and gets himself fully dressed and begins talking immediately, barely taking breaths between his sentences. On mornings when we have something special going on, he's often up *before* dawn. Like today. Even though I know this about him, and I adore his gusto, I haven't quite gotten used to it.

Before becoming a mother, I'd revel in waking up in silence, slowly, listening to the birds chirping and the river rushing and the sound of my own breath. And then maybe I'd make some coffee and write for a couple of hours. Or I'd practice yoga, or go for a run in the foothills.

But motherhood means waking up on call every day; answering questions and changing diapers and pouring yogurt and cereal into bowls, making sure to pour them in the right order, so that Jake or Elise—it could be either—doesn't freak out and scream, "I wanted the cereal *under* the yogurt," which creates a whole new level of demands and discussions that go in circles. Part of me loves the raw energy my kids emanate, and part of me longs for the peace of my past.

Chris rolls over, puts his arm around me, and pipes in. "Jake, go play in your room for a while. We'll get up soon."

Jake sighs. "Ohhhh," he whines.

"Go," Chris says.

I hear Jake trudging down the stairs, muttering to himself.

"And don't wake up your sister!"

Chris pulls me close and kisses my neck. "Mmmm," I say. We lay curled in each other's heat, silky skin interwoven with smooth sheets, and I sigh. He falls asleep almost immediately. I admire his ability to do this—sleep anywhere, anytime—something that has become elusive for me since becoming a mother. I fidget and turn and consider getting out of bed and then turn over again. Jake mentioned camping, and now I can't stop thinking about it.

We're about to embark on a three-day backpacking trip near Cameron Pass, high up in the Colorado mountains, close to the yurt we visited when Jake was a newborn, when I came to terms with my postpartum depression and committed to revising my fantasy of motherhood. This is our first backpacking trip with two kids—Elise has just turned two–and it feels like it's been a long time coming. I'm more than ready. It's early fall, a perfect time to camp in Colorado, when the weather is mild and the leaves of the Cottonwoods and Aspen glow bright yellow, like flames among pine. I'm so excited to be together as a family in the wilderness for more than a day hike, to watch Jake and Elise together in the woods, to see what they notice and how they interact.

On the other hand, I'm totally overwhelmed by the effort this type of family adventure requires. My mind races with myriad thoughts: *I hate hauling diapers. The weather is always unpredictable in the mountains. What if it hails? Elise hates her car seat. Jake promised he won't whine, but he probably will, and I hate whining. Maybe we should stay home and just go to the neighborhood park. That would be easier. Parks have trees and grass, right?*

But, no. I force my body into action, untangling from Chris, pushing up on my elbows and swinging my legs over the side of the bed, standing up and stretching my arms over my head. A few more rays of sunlight peek through the blinds, fueling my efforts. I turn and look at Chris. "You ready to do this?" I ask.

He flips his eyes open. "What?"

"Camping?"

He yawns. "Oh, it's so early. You sure you want to go?"

I smile. "Yes."

"Positive?"

"Come on. Get up." Recently, I read an inspirational quote about how a person can choose to be an innovator or a martyr. It struck me, because it's something I've thought about a lot, especially in terms of parenting. Parents can either figure out how to be happy, or they can sit around making excuses. It's easier to make excuses, and I hate when I catch myself being the martyr. Today, I won't.

I think of my friend who lives in California with her husband and two young daughters. She's a badass ex-whitewater river guide who's led trips all over the world. Now that she has kids, she finds running them down Class II and III rapids as thrilling as guiding Class V ever was, but gathering the energy and time to pack up not only the trip gear (boats, paddles, pumps, coolers, First Aid kits), but all the kid gear (sippy cups, diapers, back-up pajamas, sunhats, sunscreen) is her biggest challenge. She's had to let go of the expectation that she can throw together her kit the day before the trip, like she did pre-kids.

This morning, I'm in the same boat as my friend. While Chris lies on his back staring at the ceiling, trying hard to wake up, I head downstairs to our camping gear closet. Our food is already packed and ready to go, a plethora of cheese, bagels, summer sausage, freeze-dried meals, raisins, chocolate chips, and dried mangos stored in the fridge and zippered into bags in the kitchen. But some stuff still needs packing.

Jake appears at my side. "Hi Mommy, you decided to get up!" he says.

"Yep." I pull open the closet door. While Jake gabs, I collect gear out of boxes and off shelves. Into the pile go fleece jackets, rain suits, three-person tent, headlamps, a stove, and a whopping *four* sleeping bags. "Four sleeping bags," I say. "That's a lot."

"Cozy!" Jake exclaims, leaping into the pile.

I laugh. It's awesome he's this excited, and I decide to harness his enthusiasm. "Hey, Jake. Can you go grab the bag of diapers out of the bathroom?"

"Sure!" He scampers away.

Elise appears in the doorway, wearing leopard-print footie pajamas and toting a baby doll, her favorite toy. She looks adorable. "Hey, love," I say, my heart melting into a puddle of sweet liquid.

She stares at me silently. I take in her frowsy blond curls and pull her in for a hug. As she rests on my shoulder, I mentally calculate how many diapers we'll need for a three-day trip: twenty, to be safe. *Damn, that's a lot.* The diapers alone will take up a third of my pack, requiring more space than the tent or the food.

A few months ago, Chris and I left the kids with my parents and took a three-night backpacking trip into the Never Summer

Wilderness, a favorite region of ours on the west side of Rocky Mountain National Park. Even though we were carrying huge packs and climbing arduous trails to 12,000 feet elevation, above timberline, it felt easier than all of the packing and planning and anticipating that happens when we go out into the wilderness with kids. At one point on the trip, when Chris and I were lazing in our tent reading books and drinking hot chocolate after a day on the trail, Chris used the word "luxurious" to describe our experience. Odd as it sounded, I had to agree. Without kids, living in a tent in the middle of nowhere was simple.

———

Today, nothing about our trip feels luxurious and when we finally arrive at the trailhead, several hours after waking up, we look sloppy, like tourists who rented some gear on a whim. As we pull everything out of the trunk, Chris and I recap our plan for the tenth time since dawn. I will carry Elise in a kid backpack with the tent and tarp fastened to the lower bars. Chris will carry his overstuffed pack, which must weigh somewhere around sixty pounds. Jake has promised to walk without whining—it's his first hike of this distance wearing his own backpack containing water and snacks.

As we begin hiking, I think, *One foot in front of the other*. Elise, who is sucking on a lollipop, leans wildly to one side of the pack, then the other, pushing me off balance in various directions. The tent didn't fasten as solidly to the bars of my pack as we'd anticipated, so it's hanging slightly askew, pushing me even further off center. Chris looks like an elf under his enormous pack. He puffs loudly. Jake ambles along, chatting.

Ten minutes later, Jake has still not stopped talking. He fires off a string of questions in his little kid way, things that have no logical or definite answer: "Will we see any animals? What lives inside that log? Why do your hiking boots squeak when you walk? Are there big fish in the river? What if a bear comes into our tent? Where, exactly, do the moose live?"

In the background, Elise sings a shrill version of "Twinkle, Twinkle, Little Star" into my ear.

I stop and take a long, deep breath. I stretch my arms out to the side. "Jake and Elise," I say. "Shhh. Listen."

Jake looks up at me. "What, Mommy?"

"Shhh," I say. "What do you hear?"

For one long, beautiful moment, it is completely silent.

Jake shrugs. "I don't hear anything."

Elise kicks me in the lower back and resumes singing.

"Wait," I say.

I grab Elise's foot with one hand, and Jake's hand with my other. "Let's walk in silence for a while. Just to notice what we hear. And hey, if we're loud we will scare the animals and then we won't see them."

This seems to intrigue Jake—he peers into the forest excitedly—and although I can't see Elise's face, she's completely quiet.

Chris points to a stick. "Jake, grab that," he says. "You can use it to protect us."

Jake's eyes light up. He picks up the stick and shakes it around in the air. "My light saber," he says. I didn't know he knew what a light saber was. Has he even seen *Star Wars*? Either way, he seems thrilled to have a job, and that's good enough.

We begin walking again and I revel in the voices of nature: the quaking of aspen leaves, my boots slapping rock, birds chirping in the trees, insects clicking in the underbrush. I touch a velvety leaf to my cheek, run Elise's toe across the rough bark of a pine. She squeals with delight.

This little break, this pause to integrate into our surroundings, seems to have calmed everyone down and curbed nervous energy. As we trudge together, I look around at our family. Our little backpacking family—Jake walking in his tiny boots, and Elise riding along and Chris and I carrying everything we need on our backs. Jake points to logs that look like animals, peers through the trees for elk, and searches for Y-shaped sticks that would make good slingshots. I beam. This makes me so proud. We're doing this. I thought it might be impossible, but we're here. We're backpacking with kids! It's wonderful in the present moment, and it also opens doors to many possibilities. The idea of traveling further into the wide world as a family makes my heart thump with joy.

The first mile takes more than an hour. It's slow. We stop a lot. Jake requests snacks every few minutes, and I take a stash of goldfish-shaped crackers out of my pocket; a treat he rarely gets at home. Near the summit another hour later, Jake complains that his "bottom hurts." He begins to whine in earnest. I can't blame him. My bottom hurts too. As do my shoulders and lower back.

"We're so close, buddy," I say. I hold his hand, urging him on.

Jake stands there, unwilling to move. I pull out my last card: I remind him of his mission, which is to deliver an important note to the top of the mountain.

For Jake's fourth birthday, Chris built him a playhouse made out of recycled materials: retired fence posts, found logs, discarded flooring. The escape hatch is made from a slide he picked up at a used home improvement store. It's adorable, beautiful handiwork. We organized a "Playhouse Warming Party," inviting all of Jake's friends, and the neighbor boy brought a mailbox to add to his playhouse. This inspired Chris and me to invent a series of imaginary friends for Jake—the Playhouse Animals: deer, raccoon, eagle, hawk, bear—who would exchange letters with him in his mailbox. On the morning of our trip, Jake found a note in his box that said:

Dear Jake,

My baby needs an important medicine. But only the owl on the top of the mountain can get it and deliver it to me. Can you send him this message?

Love, Playhouse Deer

This reminder is *the* reason Jake makes it to the top of the mountain. Chris and I exchange a congratulatory look, although I give Chris most of the credit. He built the playhouse and does most of the letter-writing.

⸻

As we set up camp in a pretty meadow, peaks looming in the distance, I stop to wipe the sweat off my forehead and stretch my achy back. Jake and Elise play under a canopy of fir and spruce, pretending to be beavers, building a house and looking for food. They scurry all around, talking in hushed voices, and then come together inside their house, huddling together and pretending to eat. Out here, their imaginations are running as wild as the landscape. Later, they straddle a log that's their "horse." Climb a rock that's a rocket ship. Swim in the "sea" of tall, pale grass.

The daylight fades and I begin building a fire while Chris looks for a good spot to hang the food bag, out of reach from bears.

Jake starts getting nervous. "The scary animals come out now, Mommy," he says, eyes big, staring into the distance.

Elise looks terrified. And then the most fascinating thing happens. Elise picks up a three-pronged branch and begins to rock it like a baby. It looks nothing, of course, like her doll that's home in her bedroom, yet she feeds and rocks this pretend infant, humming softly; her way of finding comfort in a place that's full of unknowns. It's beautiful.

"Come here, Lulu," I say, using my nickname for Elise. "And you too, Jakey."

They wander over. I snuggle Jake and Elise and Baby Stick in my lap. Together, we sing "Twinkle, Twinkle, Little Star" while looking up at the stars.

Chris sits down and joins our little sing-along. "I love you guys so much," he says. "I love that we're doing this."

"Me too," I say.

"Me three," Jake and Elise say in unison. They giggle.

We sit together, snug and safe—one.

I think back to the morning, when I was lying in bed, stalling, focused on all of the excuses not to do this trip. I'm glad I swung my legs over the edge of the bed and overcame, because these kinds of moments, rich with layers, are invaluable. A good reminder to occasionally trek beyond the neighborhood park.

Where I Began

Five Years, Four Months into Motherhood

I am lost in Rome. For the last hour, I've been trying to convince myself otherwise. *This alley looks familiar. Surely this cobblestone path will cross a main street. I can't be that far from a tourist booth.* But now the river is here and Colosseum is where? And how did these ancient ruins appear on the side of the street? Fiats speed by. A Vespa whizzes so close I stumble backwards.

I pull my purse closer to my side, puff out my cheeks, blow out air, and continue walking. My boots slap the cement sidewalk. Inside, I fume. When I travel solo, I'm adamant about safety. Which means, in part, not getting lost. This is my sixth day in Rome, and every day I've been so diligent—wandering around with my map, tucking away landmarks in my head, memorizing the neighborhoods and layout of streets. No small feat in a city that's world-renowned for its twisting, maze-like properties. I was doing really well.

But today I am map-less, and it's because I got caught up. I shared a long breakfast with Francesca, the woman who owns the *pension* I'm staying at a few miles from the city center, and I was captivated by her story. She's a single mom who had her daughter in her early forties. Before becoming a mother, she traveled all over the world, to Cuba, Egypt, and Argentina, but a new baby urged her to settle down. However, she did something unique to keep the spark alive: she bought this little inn, which provides both a steady source of income and adventure. She gets to meet people from all over the world, which encourages her to daydream about the places she and her daughter will visit together when the time is right. I found our conversation so energizing, my mind bursting with ideas (maybe Chris and I should buy a B&B! Or parlay our skills to work remotely!), that I left my room without my map. I can see it lying there, crumpled, on my bedside table.

And now, here I am, alone, lost in Rome like the woman in Woody Allen's film *To Rome with Love*.

"*Disculpe,*" I say to a woman toting two toddler boys with impossibly beautiful thick black hair. "*Um, donde es…*"

She wrinkles up her forehead.

I realize I'm speaking Spanish in Italy, but a couple of friends said the two languages are similar enough that I might be able to get by.

I close my eyes, trying to grab the right phrase out of my brain. Both Spanish and German words spin like a tornado, which for me is the result of knowing a little bit of both languages, but not being fluent in either.

I try again. "*Yo busco Trev…*"

One of the toddlers whacks the other one on the arm, crying

ensues, and their mother turns away, spewing a litany of harsh-sounding words.

"Um, never mind," I say to her back.

I was trying to ask her where to find the Trevi Fountain, a landmark I know well. I look up the street, and then down. Nothing looks familiar. Exasperated, I turn on my heel, determined to re-trace my steps and figure out where I went wrong. At this point, I just want to go back home. *This trip was a stupid idea*, I think. *Why am I even here?*

Unlike most people who visit Rome, I'm not here to visit the Vatican or any of the other "Top 10 Sights." I'm not here to take side trips to Florence or Venice. I'm here, walking around seemingly aimlessly, looking for something intangible: a dream.

For more than a dozen years, I've had a recurring dream that won't leave me alone. It starts with me walking through a long, narrow basement that is dimly lit. Shelves of boxes covered in sheets line the sides. I run my fingers along scratchy black material, feeling curious, taking it all in. At the far end of the room, there's a small door, and streaks of sunlight shine through, dust floating in the air like fairies. I have to bend over to push open the door, and when I do, I enter a crumbling cement patio. There's a water-stained birdbath, an empty stone swimming pool, a fountain, and a stone lion head sculpture hanging on the wall. The light is soft. My breath is slow. I wander, mesmerized, touching the cool stone and wondering who lived there. My entire body melts into the space, as if I become part of it. I feel soft and peaceful.

Whenever I tell people about the dream, which is not often, I try to downplay its significance. "Oh, it's very *Lion, Witch, and the Wardrobe*," I say, quickly changing the subject. I've never wanted the dream analyzed, because it feels like it's meant only for me, and I don't want people saying things like, "the stone lion probably represents your ego," or, "the empty pool probably mirrors your loneliness." Maybe these things are true, but I want to find out for myself.

When I was hiking the Paria canyon, trying to get to know my companions early in the trip, before things got miserable, I told them about the dream. Out there, in the wide open, I exposed my secret to two men I barely knew. They didn't analyze it. One of them simply said, "That sounds like Rome."

His words struck me, because I'd been feeling drawn to visiting Rome, even though the Italian countryside seemed a more natural fit for my personality. On a whim, not sure it was a good use of the money I'd been tucking away for two years—little bits I'd gotten for holidays or my birthday—I booked a ticket. Chris was supportive, but also a little bummed. Italy was a place he also wanted to visit. I promised him I'd check things out—scout the area—and come up with some ideas for returning as a couple, or a family.

Today, as I wander, trying to find anything familiar, I think about how I'm almost halfway through my trip, and I haven't found anywhere that even remotely resembles the dream. My first day, walking around, I realized the entire city screams, "Power! Virility! Dominance! Chaos!" You can practically smell the blood of dead beasts in the air, impaled by ancient warriors in the Colosseum, and it's nearly impossible to cross the street without getting hit. My dream isn't anything like this. Comparatively, it's like a little white lamb grazing in a field. Or a soft cotton blanket. Or a Greek goddess. Maybe I should be in

Greece? *Shit, I should be in Greece! Or at least Tuscany, where there is open space.*

I stride over a cobblestone path which has no cars. A young woman paints in oil on canvas outside a small gallery. A man in a suit stands in the arched doorway of a café. He nods.

"Buongiorno," I say. Above me, I hear voices cascading out of open windows. I hear people say, *Pronto,* a*llora.* There's a giggle. The cry of a child.

It makes me think of my own children. Still, when I travel solo and I hear or see children, it tugs at my heart. Just like in Turkey, when I was walking with Abdul and the kids on the steps reminded me of Jake, pulling me off balance. The longing and guilt is the hardest part. It has never gotten easier.

Except on the night before I left on this trip, I had an illuminating conversation with Jake. We were sitting at the dinner table, and he'd just asked for the millionth time, "Mommy, why do you have to leave?" Of course, I didn't *have to* leave. Which made me feel even more guilty for leaving. And selfish. So I kept repeating various forms of the same answer: *I'm just going on a little solo trip. I'll be back before you know it.*

Every time, his eyes would cloud over in confusion, and then he'd repeat the question. "But why?" he'd ask. Finally, I decided to try a new approach. I took his hand and led him to the giant world map on his wall. We sat on the floor.

First, I traced the arc my plane would fly, from Denver to Philadelphia to Rome. He marveled at the size of the Atlantic Ocean and the funny boot-like shape of Italy. Then we talked about passion, and what it means to support others. I told him I was born with something called wanderlust, which has become stronger as I've gotten older. I need to travel to feel happy. When I travel alone, I see things in a new way, talk to people I'd generally not even notice, and rely on my inner voice. This inspires me. It also makes me a better mom, because I return home feeling energized.

Then I asked Jake to tell me about something he loves. He blurted, "Motorcycles."

Swallowing the image of Evel Knievel, I told him that someday he might like to save money and buy his own bike. He might want to race it, or travel off-road, or attend rallies. If it's something he's passionate about, I'll support him. He lit up. "Oh, I get it!" he exclaimed.

I really think he did. For the first time, Jake understood in a tangible way the concept of identity. Even better, my solo trip to Rome *prompted* the discussion, putting theory into practice in a positive way. For the first time, I saw how my adventures were actually positively impacting my children. Elise wasn't old enough to have this discussion yet, but she would be soon. It was thrilling to watch the door to future conversations open wide.

I thought of my friend, a painter, who has three school-aged boys. One day she admitted to me that she got lost completely along the motherhood journey, consumed with her boys, unable to remember who she was as an individual. She had to hit just about bottom in order to reach for her paintbrushes again and make getting in the art room a priority. But she learned that even painting for an hour, during the day or in the middle of the night, created such a shift toward feeling whole. Always, she had to work past the guilt of taking that kind of time for herself. But interestingly, she's noticed that the more she paints, the more proud her boys are of her. The more they want to learn. The more they respect her.

Kids respect their parents for being individuals. That's what I keep telling myself as I wander lost in Rome, berating myself. I enter an alley and hear the clinking of silverware and smell the zesty aroma of a red sauce simmering on a stove. Somehow, it's already lunchtime. My stomach growls. Perhaps a plate of pasta will reorient me, or at least curb my disappointment. The narrow street opens up into a small piazza—the little hand-lettered sign says "Piazza Margana"—and I see people gathering in a wine bar. I request a table for one, order wine, pull out my notebook and take some notes about being lost. I look up at the table next to me. It's a group of four—two women in their late forties, and two teenaged girls. They are laughing and chatting, their shopping bags shoved under the table. It must be a mother-daughter trip. I think of Francesca and her daughter, and of me and Elise. These incredible opportunities we have as parents to show our kids the world.

I take some more notes, and when I look up, the women are staring at me. One of them points to an empty chair. "Join us?" she asks in an accent that sounds Irish.

I look around, in case she's talking to someone else, but it appears that she means me. I smile. "Sure."

I join the women at the table, and they introduce themselves: Ginny and Fiona, and their daughters. They are from Glasgow, Scotland.

"We invited you over because you reminded us of that actress from that show *Sex and the City,*" Fiona announces. "Are you from New York?"

I look down. Although I'm wearing a dusty rose dress and

trendy belt—being in the city has inspired me to replace my typical yoga pant and tunic uniform with hip dresses and boots and skinny jeans, which feels so feminine and lovely—I don't look like any of the actresses on that show. Or any actress at all. And even though I've been asked a dozen times if I'm from New York City, it's only because all of the Europeans I've met think there are only three states in the United States: New York, California, and the state of mind, Las Vegas.

But *Sex and the City* is how our connection is established: Over a show about women and sex in a city in America that I've only visited once, but they assume I know well. Over wine and pizza, I relax as we talk about the American actors they think are dreamy, and the upcoming presidential election, which has them on edge, and our favorite places, so far, in Rome.

"So, are you here alone?" Ginny asks.

I nod. Normally, I tense up when someone asks me this question, but around these women I feel comfortable. Still, I assume they will question my intentions.

But they don't. "Good for you!" says Ginny. She looks at her daughter. "See, this is something you could do too when you get a little older."

Her daughter smiles at me.

"I've always traveled," she says. "Even when my kids were little."

"Really?" I ask, overly enthusiastic, excited for her to elaborate.

She tells so many interesting stories about her excellent adventures, near and far. And then, as if on cue, she mentions childcare. (I'd been wondering how she pulled it off.) But Ginny, being the innovator she is, did something novel. She didn't have an easier childcare arrangement than anyone else, so she started a childcare program in her neighborhood. She made some paper vouchers, representing time. Each family started with a certain number of vouchers, and then they'd exchange them for babysitting.

"It was so freeing," says Ginny.

Wow, I think. *No martyrdom for this woman.* I listen, rapt, learning from Ginny, my mind racing with ideas and optimism.

When they say they need to get back to their hotel, I'm not ready to go. But we exchange email addresses and promise to keep in touch. I doubt that we will, just like I haven't with Abdul, or most others, but even so, I like adding them to my global community. To the list of people with whom I've connected deeply.

As the women walk away, I notice from the light it is late afternoon—totally gorgeous—and my eyes are drawn to a second-floor balcony which is overgrown with lush vines and flowers and plants. "That's beautiful," I whisper. I could see myself sitting on that balcony, writing or reading. I take photo after photo, capturing the space.

And then I turn to my right, and I see an arched doorway. The green doors are pushed open, and inside is a tunnel-like alley leading to somewhere. Where? I crane my neck and gaze down the dim hallway. At the end, I see a stone lion perched over a fountain. *Whoa.*

My movements happen automatically: I walk inside, even though it's a private entrance, mesmerized, touching everything I can—the smooth, cool walls, a marble sculpture of a nude man, the slippery foliage, the trickling water. Light filters down from the tall roof. It's quiet. Birds chirp. The air smells like water.

I kneel down and run my hands along the cobblestones. Cup the curved stone. I sit on a ledge near the fountain, reach out my arm, and watch the water run over my fingers. A tingling runs through me, from my fingertips down to my heart, belly, pelvis, toes. Everything is reminiscent. The light. The cracked patio. The lion. *This feeling.* There is no question: This is the place from my dream.

I take dozens of photos, because I know a security officer may appear at any moment and ask me to leave. And in the next days, I try to make logical sense of the space. I research the Margana family, the namesake of the piazza, and wonder if there might be some connection to my Italian family. I scour ancestry.com for answers. I search the Internet for Piazza Margana and learn that long ago it was a place where artists showed their work, which inspired the Tor Margana award for artists, still in existence. Maybe I'm related to a famous artist? I scrutinize the details of the photos, looking for answers.

When I go back to the piazza, I find the doors to the fountain locked. I stand outside, analyzing my surroundings. I think that maybe the lion symbolizes C.S. Lewis' Aslan, God, or my husband, because his astrological sign is Leo. All of this seems far-fetched, a desperate stretch of my imagination. None of it resonates.

So I take a step back. I sit down and press my back against the wall and feel the ripples of brick massaging into my shoulders. I close my eyes. I stop thinking. And I ponder the same question I did during Elise's birth: *What do I know?*

What I know is this: The space moves me. I feel touched by the painters and writers of the past who worked diligently in this place and offered their creations to the world. Today, in the piazza, there are earnest workers: a maid in a blue pinstriped dress shaking out a rug, a female server running her restaurant, a security officer sweeping up leaves, a man in an open window hunched over a desk.

And I realize the symbolism runs deeper than I knew. Piazza Margana, and the quiet cove, are places of peace within chaos. Silence within the fray. It evokes my intuition. Simplicity. And of course, it's not a coincidence that I needed to forget my map in order to find this place, or that it happened after inspiring conversations with Francesca and Ginny and Fiona. These women—my tribe—led me here.

I take all of this as a reminder to continue following my authentic wild self and not to get swept up in the chaos. When I listen to external messages, it pulls me from my core. When I feel lured to be someone I'm not—a mother who makes perfect crafts or obsesses over the right preschool or that feels selfish for indulging my adventurous spirit—I must find a place where I can let that all go. To be myself is enough. This place in a piazza in Italy represents where I began; who I was when I was born. Naked. Unclouded. Perfect.

But how will I report this to my family and friends? The epiphany feels important but will seem anti-climactic (even crazy) to others. They will say, "Show me your pictures!" Yet I don't have the ones they want to see.

Maybe I should lie? Or I'll just give vague updates. But there's one person I'll tell the real truth to: Jake, my young son. I think of the conversation we had the night before I left, when we talked about identity.

When Jake's attention began waning, I pulled out his Kindergarten calendar and circled the day I'd be back from

Rome. It would be "Bat Day" in his classroom, for the proximity to Halloween. He thought this was fantastic. Rome was important to me, Halloween was important to him, and we'd reunite with exciting stories to tell.

And so that is what we'll do. He'll tell me all about Bat Day, and I'll tell him how I found a place with a lion that made me remember who I am. I will tell him to always be himself. I will tell him that sometimes getting lost is the only way to be found.

Epilogue

Almost Six Years into Motherhood

It's mid-morning on a Wednesday, and I grab my children's favorite book off the tile countertop in our Mexican *casa*. As I stare down at the gangly, furry moose on the cover, I feel a sudden tingling sensation on my hands. "What?" I say, squinting, and then, "Gross!" My fingers are covered in ants. I toss the book on the floor, wildly shaking my wrists.

Jake and Elise, ages five and two, come running from their bedroom wearing their swimsuits, because we are about to walk to the beach. They stare down at the book. Jake furrows his eyebrows. I can see his mind questioning, calculating, deducing. "Elise," he says. "Get a stick."

She obeys, running to the porch, her bottom jiggling in her swimsuit. I hear her rifling through the bits of nature they've collected on walks: leaves, seashells, *cocos*. She brings back two sticks, because she is not one to be left out of anything, especially an adventure. They both stand over the book, poking around. A ray of sunshine illuminates the cover like a spotlight.

"Stay back," I say, glancing at the papery skin of their feet. "Ants bite."

Jake's stick stops on the moose's hoof. "Look," he says, his voice serious. "Do you see that?" He bends down closer. "Is it salsa?"

I get down on my hands and knees, but not too close, because the ants are now crawling around chaotically, trying to avoid being gouged. I push away a few grains of sand, and lean forward. "Oh," I say, drawing out the word. "You're right." In fact, there's a dollop of dried red sauce on the cover of the book—the culprit—probably from yesterday, or the day before. The tiniest spill, and the jungle moved in.

We've been living in Yelapa, Mexico, for just over a month—our family of four tucked into a three-room abode on a cobblestone path near the shores of the Pacific Ocean. Our house is stripped down to simple; from the kids' hand-drawn pictures that decorate our walls to the candles we made out of plastic cups and sand to our shower that spews only cold water. Our washing machine is a big outdoor sink. The windows are wide open. Sometimes the air smells like sewer or burning trash, but mostly it's pleasantly aromatic—hinting at whatever delectable recipe our neighbor is cooking while clanking around in her kitchen. Tamales? Tortillas? Huevos rancheros? Bits of culture floating in through our nostrils and ears.

We wipe up the salsa with a damp rag and start off on the dirt path to the beach. I leave a hand-written note for Chris, who is in a Skype meeting with his office back home. *Going to Isabel's Beach. Join us?*

The neighbor woman waves down from her balcony. "*Hola, Princesa,*" she says to Elise.

"*Hola,*" Elise responds. A few days ago, it seems that the Spanish language began to click for her. She plods forward, while Jake runs ahead.

"Mommy, I walk," she says, looking back at me proudly. I can tell she is trying so hard to concentrate, but there are so many things to look at: pelicans, the waves of the ocean, people passing by on foot or horseback. I give her the time and space to check everything out, and it gives me a rare chance, too. I run my fingers over the reddish bark of a tree, marvel at a leaf that is four times the size of my hand, and scan the cove for humpback whales.

When Elise and I arrive at the beach, Jake is standing on a boulder. "The sea is calm today," he says, and it's true. The tide is low at the moment, and the shallow water is blue-green, the surf gently folding over onto the beach. I think about how interesting it is to be here for an extended period, so we can observe the ebb and flow of the sea, something we can't do at home in the mountains, or on shorter vacations. Jake keeps tabs, enhancing the Kindergarten lessons we brought from home to keep him up to speed.

Out of nowhere, a Canadian girl appears, and then a collection of Mexican boys. Without speaking, the kids all set to work digging a giant hole in the sand, communicating through hand gestures and facial expressions. I take some notes in my journal. I record how present I feel. How lovely it is to observe my children embracing a new environment. How I love to look out over the water and not see giant high-rise buildings and condos. Yelapa is part of an indigenous land trust, so only native Yelapans can own the land, keeping things traditional.

An acquaintance of mine, an artist, told me she's found a place inside herself where creativity and motherhood work together. Up until this moment, I couldn't imagine this was possible, especially for myself. For so long my life has felt compartmentalized, almost like I've been more than one person. But now, I sense what she's talking about. Here in Yelapa, immersed in all of my roles–writer, mom, wife, traveler–I feel a strong synergy.

I look up the hill and spot Chris walking toward us. His face looks happy, and he carries a plastic bag that appears to be bursting with a picnic. He plops down next to me and puts his arms around my shoulders and I snuggle into him. "How was work?" I ask.

"Everything was good at the office," he says.

He looks genuinely pleased that things aren't falling apart without him physically sitting at his desk in Colorado; that it's possible to keep in touch with his staff, and check To Do items off his list, from all these miles away.

Jake and Elise taunt Chris from the water. "Daddy, come swimming," they say. They run in circles, beckoning him over.

"Why not," he says, a phrase he's begun using the last few weeks, a beautiful diversion from The List, which naturally was his initial reaction when I proposed doing this trip. But something has changed. He stands up and peels off his shirt, and I stare at his body, strong and tanned. I take in his huge smile and soft eyes and watch him pick up both kids in his arms, pretending to be a bear. Over the last month his entire face has softened, and he laughs easier and plays harder with the kids. I think about how sexy this is, how I'm glad I didn't ride away with another man in a moment of impulse, because the man I want is right here. He has always been here.

He looks back at me. "Come swimming," he says.

I crinkle up my face. "Are there jellies?" I ask, referring to the jellyfish that sometimes hang out in this cove. He shrugs and looks in the water. "I don't know. Come on!"

Fully aware that the tables have turned—that he's the one prodding me—and liking it, I stand up. "Let's go."

As we play in the waves, tossing a ball around, I start having pangs about leaving Yelapa, even though it's still a few weeks away. I look at Chris and ask, "Would you ever do this again?" I bite my lip and hold the ball to my chest.

"I'd love to."

"What has happened to you?" I ask, jokingly. "Where did my husband go?"

He tells me that our time in Yelapa has helped him overcome his fears about living in a new, very different place. He felt insecure walking through the village at first, but now he has to allow extra time to get somewhere, because he stops and talks to people along the way, or buys something from a *tienda,* or lingers to stare at a pretty bird or butterfly. He's exploring further and loving it. It's a nice complement to the synergy I'm feeling.

I beam. "Do you think we can pull it off?" I ask. "Maybe even another extended trip?"

"Why not?"

I look out at the water and embrace this moment, because we've worked so hard for it. I imagine all the milestones on the adventure list—the developmental stages of parenthood–a beautiful visual representation of how we've forged this authentic life as a family.

I look at Chris and smile. "You're right," I say. "Why not?"

Acknowledgements

This book is a celebration of the wild human spirit, and I'm grateful for the community that surrounded me during its creation.

A huge thanks to Chris Lavergne, Mink Choi, Kaitlyn Wylde, Daniella Urdinlaiz, Mark Kupasrimonkol, Nick Kinling, and Melissa Ximena for your excitement in sharing this project with the world, and for your incredible talent and tenacity.

Kate Johnson, I feel fortunate every day for your brilliance, energy and frame-able emails.

Dana Masden, thanks for saying, "I think you might be writing a book here," that one day in writers' group when you were critiquing one of my essays. And also for your unwavering support.

Thank you to Janet Freeman, Bonnie Nadzam, Laura Resau, Laura Pritchett, and Karye Cattrell for reading various versions of the manuscript and offering excellent feedback.

Dr. Betsy Hirsch, I will forever be grateful to you for pulling me into your office during graduate school and encouraging me on my quest for self.

It was an honor to work with Dr. Naomi Rachel and Johannah Racz when I first decided I wanted to be a writer.

Wild spirits unite! I'm grateful to all the people who inspired this book and who contributed advice.

Thanks to my parents and sister for raising me wild and for teaching me how to use my voice.

And finally, a big thank you to my husband, Chris. This book would not exist without his love, patience, and questionable sense of humor.

About the Author

Carrie Visintainer is a freelance writer and the founder of Free Your Wild, empowering people to unlock and embrace their personal "wild." She received an M.S. in molecular biology and genetics from the University of Minnesota. This is her first book.

Credits

"Solo on a Spare" appeared in the Travelers' Tales *The Best Women's Travel Writing 2008* anthology and "Sidecar Sally" in the same anthology in 2012.

A version of "Culture Shock" appeared in the Write for Charity *From the Heart: A Collection of Stories and Poems from the Front Lines of Parenting* anthology.

Versions of "Under the Microscope" appeared in *Proto* and *Ars Medica.*

"One Moment in Life" appeared in *MaMaZinA* online.

"Wild Mama" (published as "The Snobbiest Mommy on the Block") appeared in *Fort Collins Magazine.*